SAVOURY PIES & PUDDINGS

by
Anne Chamberlain

Edited by
Carolyn Humphries

foulsham
London · New York · Toronto · Sydney

foulsham
The Publishing House, Bennetts Close,
Cippenham, Slough, Berkshire, SL1 5AP

ISBN 0-572-02141-0

Printed in Great Britain at
Cox & Wyman Ltd, Reading, Berkshire.

CONTENTS

INTRODUCTION

Imagine crisp, crumbly shortcrust encasing layers of flavoursome root vegetables and tangy farmhouse cheese. Or flaky filo leaves gathered neatly around a cutlet of succulent salmon. Picture the golden elegance of traditional steak and kidney pie or the cool freshness of a savoury summer pudding. From firm old favourites to exciting new ideas, *Savoury Pies and Puddings* will give you sumptuous recipes for every occasion. Whether you are planning to picnic in the sun, entertain in style, knock up a quick supper snack or create an elaborate centerpiece for a party, you'll find the perfect recipe in this book.

Wrapping simple or exotic ingredients in pastry not only traps all the flavours, it makes them go further too. And even if after following our instructions you don't feel up to pastry making you don't have to. Most types are available ready made or frozen from your local supermarket so you can make mouthwatering masterpieces any time with hardly any effort at all!

* All recipes marked with * can be frozen.

ALL ABOUT PASTRY

Pastry-making is not difficult, but it is important to follow a few basic rules. Except for hot-water and choux pastry, keep all ingredients cool and work in cool conditions. Use good fresh ingredients and weigh them carefully. Bake at the correct temperatures, and you should always find your pastry is perfect.

Ingredients
Use plain (all-purpose) flour for the best results. For puff pastry, use strong plain (bread) flour which helps to keep the flaky layers in the pastry. Always use the proportion of fat to flour given in the recipe, as too little will make pastry hard, and too much will make it very 'short' and unmanageable. Hard fats are better than the soft varieties.

Method for Shortcrust (Basic Pie Crust)
Fat should not be over-rubbed into the flour as this makes the pastry break when rolled out. Rub it in lightly with fingers and thumbs until the mixture is like fine breadcrumbs. Very little water is necessary to mix the pastry – usually about 3 tablespoons chilled water to 225g/8 oz/2 cups flour. This should be added all at once and the dough should be firm but not sticky. A little more will be needed for wholemeal, (graham) flour.

Rolling

Roll out the pastry on a cool surface, preferably on a marble slab or enamel table, and handle it as little as possible. If the pastry is shaped into an approximate square, rectangle, circle or oval before rolling, it will save unnecessary handling. Always turn the pastry not the rolling pin for even rolling.

Trimming and Fitting

Lift the pastry on the rolling pin to put it into a container, or over a filling, but do not stretch the pastry or it will shrink again during cooking. For single crust deep pies, roll pastry out to about 5 cm/2 in larger than the dish. Cut off a strip all round. Dampen rim of dish and lay strip on. Dampen again before laying 'lid' on top. Knock up (raise up) edge with the back of a knife then flute or crimp edge to decorate. Re-roll the trimmings to make decorations and attach them to the pie with a little water or beaten egg. Brush pastry with a little egg or milk to glaze. Cut a small hole or slit in the lid to allow steam to escape.

Baking

Preheat the oven before putting in the pie, and if possible put a metal baking sheet on the oven shelf during this time. The pie can then be put on to this hot metal which will spread the heat evenly and cook the base. Bake in the centre or at the top of the oven. If the pastry browns too quickly, cover with foil or greaseproof paper.

Baking Blind

A pastry case may be partly or completely baked before filling, and this is known as baking blind. Line the uncooked pastry case with foil or greaseproof paper and fill with baking beans, rice or crusts of bread so that the bottom does not rise during cooking. If preferred, prick the base with a fork and line with foil, but do not use beans, etc. Take this lining out about 5 minutes before the end of cooking, to allow the base to become firm.

You can bake a pastry case in the microwave in a microwave-safe container. Prick base. Lay a sheet of kitchen paper over the pastry and cook on HIGH for 2–4 minutes, depending on power out put. Remove paper and return to oven for a few seconds more to dry crust. The pastry won't brown, but once the filling is in, it won't show!

Basic Recipes

The following recipes serve as guides to the ingredients and methods used for most pastry. To calculate the finished weight of pastry, add the total flour and fats and any other weighed ingredients, e.g. 225 g/8 oz/2 cups flour makes about 350 g/12 oz/¾ lb shortcrust pastry. If there is a little pastry left from the recipe, use it for some individual pies, cheese straws or tartlets. Shortcrust and hotwater crust can be made very successfully with wholemeal (graham) flour (or half and half).

Shortcrust Pastry
(Basic Pie Crust)

	Metric	Imperial	American
Plain (all-purpose) flour	225 g	8 oz	2 cups
Salt	2.5 ml	½ tsp	½ tsp
Hard margarine	50 g	2 oz	¼ cup
Lard or white vegetable fat (shortening)	50 g	2 oz	¼ cup
Cold water	30-40 ml	2 - 3 tbsp	2 - 3 tbsp

Sift together flour and salt. Rub in fat until mixture resembles fine breadcrumbs. Add water and mix to a stiff dough. Turn out on to a floured board and knead lightly until smooth. Roll out to required shape and thickness.

Puff Pastry

	Metric	Imperial	American
Plain (all-purpose) flour	450 g	1 lb	4 cups
Salt	5 ml	1 tsp	1 tsp
Hard margarine	450 g	1 lb	2 cups
Lemon juice	10 ml	2 tsp	2 tsp
Water (as cold as possible)	300 ml	½ pt - 1 tbsp	1¼ cups - 1 tbsp

Sift together flour and salt. Divide margarine into four. Rub one quarter into flour and then mix to a pliable dough with lemon juice and water. Turn out on to a floured board and knead well until smooth. Rest for 15 minutes in a cool place. With 2 knives, form remaining margarine into a slab 13 cm/5 in square on a floured board. Roll dough into an oblong 28 x 15 cm/11 x 6 in. Place slab of fat on top end of dough, leaving a margin of about 1 cm/½ in along sides and top. Fold rest of dough over, placing upper edges of dough together. Brush off surplus flour.

First rolling Turn pastry round so that folded edge is on left-hand side. Press three open edges together with rolling pin to seal. Press dough across about 5 times with rolling pin to flatten. Roll out into an oblong about 30 x 15 cm/12 x 6 in keeping edges straight.

Second rolling Fold pastry in three by folding bottom third upwards and top third downwards and over to cover it. Turn so that folded edge is again on the left. Seal edges and roll out as before. Fold, turn and seal edges as before. Place pastry on floured plate in a polythene bag or wrap in foil and rest in a refrigerator for 20 minutes.

Third to sixth rollings Roll out 4 more times, always turning and sealing dough as before. Rest 20 minutes between each rolling. If any patches of fat still show, give dough another rolling. Rest dough before rolling out to 5 mm/¼ in or required thickness. Trim edges. Glaze with egg or milk before baking.

Rough Puff Pastry

	Metric	Imperial	American
Plain (all-purpose) flour	225 g	8 oz	2 cups
Salt	2.5 ml	½ tsp	½ tsp
Lard or white vegetable fat (shortening)	75 g	3 oz	⅜ cup
Hard margarine	75 g	3 oz	⅜ cup
Water	90 - 120 ml	6 - 8 tbsp	6 - 8 tbsp

Sift the flour and salt into a bowl. Cut up fat roughly into small pieces, about 5 mm/¼ in cubes. Add to flour and mix to a soft, not sticky, dough with water. Roll out on a floured board to an oblong, approximately 15 x 30 cm/6 x 12 in and fold bottom third upwards and top third downwards and over it. Turn dough so that folded edge is on left-hand side and seal edges. Roll, fold and seal edges twice more, keeping folded edge always to the left. If pastry becomes too soft, chill between rollings. Chill after rolling for at least 30 minutes before use. Roll out to required size, usually between 3–5 mm/⅛–¼ in thick. Trim edges. Glaze with egg or milk before baking.

Choux Pastry

This quantity will make up to 12 small balls or 4 larger ones. You will need double the quantity for the gougères in this book.

	Metric	*Imperial*	*American*
Plain (all-purpose) flour	*65 g*	*2 ½ oz*	*good ½ cup*
Pinch of salt			
Water	*150 ml*	*¼ pt*	*⅔ cup*
Butter or margarine	*25 g*	*1 oz*	*2 tbsp*
Egg, beaten	*1*	*1*	*1*

Sift flour and salt together onto a sheet of paper. Heat fat and water until fat melts. Add the flour all in one go and beat with a wooden spoon until mixture leaves sides of pan clean. Cool slightly then beat in egg a little at a time beating well after each addition. Mixture should be smooth and glossy but still hold it's shape. Use as required.

Hot Watercrust Pastry

	Metric	Imperial	American
Plain (all-purpose) flour	*350 g*	*12 oz*	*3 cups*
Salt	*5 ml*	*1 tsp*	*1 tsp*
Lard (shortening)	*150 g*	*5 oz*	*5/8 cup*
Milk and water mixed	*150 ml*	*1/4 pt*	*2/3 cup*

Sift flour and salt into a warm bowl. Put lard, milk and water into a pan, heat until fat melts, then bring to the boil. Pour at once into the centre of flour, and, using a wooden spoon, form into a paste. Turn out on to a lightly floured board and kneed quickly till smooth. Cover and stand in a warm place.

To mould: cut off one-third pastry for lip and decorations and keep warm. Roll out remaining pastry into a 25 cm/10 in circle, and line 15 cm/6 in greased loose-bottomed cake tin. Mould pastry from base and up sides until it is of even thickness, free from cracks and 5 mm/¼ in higher than top of tin. Or, mould pastry over base and 9 cm/3½ in up sides of a greased jar. Add filling. Roll out reserved pastry for a lid. Moisten edges with cold water. Cover pie with lid, press edges well together to seal, knock up and decorate. Brush top with beaten egg.

Bake in the centre of a hot oven, 220°C/425°F/Gas Mark 7 for ½ hour and then at 160–180°C/325–350°F/Gas Mark 3–4 for 1½ hours. Cover with foil if it becomes too brown.

SINGLE CRUST DEEP PIES

Shortcrust rough puff and puff pastry are all suitable for savoury pies made in deep earthenware or other oven proof pie dishes. The filling is often cooked before the pastry is put on and finished in the oven. To save washing up, you may wish to cook the filling in the pie dish with a foil covering, and to cool it slightly before topping with pastry and finishing baking. Since the oven will be on for some time, if this method is used, it is a good idea to cook some puddings or bake some cakes at the same time; fill up the odd spaces in the oven with baked potatoes to go with the pie, and some baked apples or other fruit which may be used as a pudding or as a breakfast dish. Alterativly, cook the filling in the microwave or a pressure cooker for quickness. If a deep single-crust pie is to be frozen, it should be prepared with cooked filling and then topped with pastry. This should be frozen uncooked and then either cooked straight from the freezer, or thawed before cooking. It is easiest to make pies for the freezer in foil dishes so that a china or ovenglass dish is not out of use for some time.

Steak and Kidney Pie

*	Metric	Imperial	American
Puff pastry	225 g	½ lb	½ lb
Plain (all-purpose) flour	25 g	1 oz	¼ cup
Salt and pepper			
Stewing steak, cubed	750 g	1½ lb	1½ lb
Ox kidney, cubed	225 g	½ lb	½ lb
Oil	30 ml	2 tbsp	2 tbsp
Medium onion, chopped	1	1	1
Button mushrooms, halved	100 g	¼ lb	¼ lb
Stock	300 ml	½ pt	1¼ cups
Bay leaf	1	1	1
Beaten egg	1	1	1

Put flour, steak and kidney and seasoning into a polythene bag and shake until the meat is coated with flour. Remove the meat and reserve flour. Heat oil and fry onion until just tender but not brown. Add meat and brown quickly on all sides. Add mushrooms and cook for 1 minute. Stir in reserved flour, then add stock and bay leaf. Bring to the boil, reduce heat, cover and simmer gently for 1½–2 hours or until meat is tender. Put meat and mushrooms into a deep pie dish, with enough gravy to half fill the dish.

Cover with pastry knock up and decorate. Brush with beaten egg, and bake at 220°C/425°F/gas mark 7 for 20 minutes. Reduce heat to 180°C/350°F/gas mark 4 and cook for a further 15 minutes until crisp, flaky and golden brown.

Marinated Beef and Mushroom Pie

*	Metric	Imperial	American
Puff pastry	*225 g*	*½ lb*	*½ lb*
Stewing beef	*450 g*	*1 lb*	*1 lb*
Madeira	*45 ml*	*3 tbsp*	*3 tbsp*
Dried mixed herbs	*2.5 ml*	*½ tsp*	*½ tsp*
Button mushrooms	*100 g*	*¼ lb*	*¼ lb*
Shallots	*225 g*	*½ lb*	*½ lb*
Stock	*60 ml*	*4 tbsp*	*4 tbsp*
Salt and pepper			
Beaten egg	*1*	*1*	*1*

Cut the steak in cubes and leave to stand in the wine and herbs while the pastry is being made. Brown the meat in a little fat; then turn it into a pie dish, along with the other ingredients. Cover with a piece of foil and cook at 180°C/350°F/gas mark 4 for approximately 1¼ hours or until tender. Remove, uncover and cool.

Cover with pastry, trim the edges and then flute with a knife. The trimmings may be used to decorate the top of the pie with pastry leaves. Brush the top of the pie with beaten egg and bake at 220°C/425°F/gas mark 7 for about 20 minutes or until risen and well browned.

Beef and Beer Pie

*	*Metric*	*Imperial*	*American*
Puff pastry	*350 g*	*12 oz*	*¾ lb*
Oil	*30 ml*	*2 tbsp*	*2 tbsp*
Large onions, chopped	*2*	*2*	*2*
Stewing beef, cubed	*750 g*	*1 ½ lb*	*1 ½ lb*
Plain (all-purpose) flour	*40 g*	*1½ oz*	*3 tbsp*
Salt and pepper			
Brown ale	*300 ml*	*½ pt*	*1¼ cups*
Water	*150 ml*	*¼ pt*	*⅔ cup*
Dried thyme	*2.5 ml*	*½ tsp*	*½ tsp*
Thinly pared rind of orange	*½*	*½*	*½*
Worcestershire sauce	*30 ml*	*2 tbsp*	*2 tbsp*
Milk or beaten egg			

Heat oil in a large pan and fry onions for 5 minutes. Toss beef in flour, seasoned with salt and pepper. Add to pan and fry for 5 minutes stirring until browned. Remove from heat. Stir in ale and water. Return to heat, bring to the boil, stirring. Add thyme and orange rind. Cover and simmer for 1½–2 hours until meat is tender. Remove rind, stir in Worcestershire sauce. Cool. Turn into a 1 litre/2 pt/5 cup pie dish.

Roll out the pastry and use to cover the pie dish. Trim and flute the edges. Brush the top of the pie with milk or beaten egg. Bake at 220°C/425°F/gas mark 7 for 25 minutes until pastry is golden brown.

Steak and Ham Pie

*	Metric	Imperial	American
Puff pastry	*225 g*	*8 oz*	*½ lb*
Chuck steak	*450 g*	*1 lb*	*1 lb*
Uncooked ham	*225 g*	*8 oz*	*½ lb*
Chopped fresh thyme	*15 ml*	*1 tbsp*	*1 tbsp*
Chopped fresh parsley	*30 ml*	*2 tbsp*	*2 tbsp*
Pinch of grated nutmeg			
Salt and pepper			
Beef stock	*450 ml*	*¾ pt*	*2 cups*
Egg yolk	*1*	*1*	*1*

Cut the beef and ham into small cubes and arrange in a pie dish. Sprinkle with herbs, nutmeg, salt and pepper. Pour on the stock. Cover with a lid or foil and cook at 180°C/350°F/gas mark 4 for 1 ½ hours. Remove the lid, and cover the dish with pastry rolled out to fit. Brush the surface with beaten egg yolk. Bake at 220°C/425°F/gas mark 7 for about 25 minutes until the pastry is golden brown.

Beef Bubble and Squeak Pie

	Metric	Imperial	American
Shortcrust pastry	225 g	8 oz	½ lb
Stewing steak	450 g	1 lb	1 lb
Large onion, thinly sliced	1	1	1
Potatoes, thinly sliced	450 g	1 lb	1 lb
Cabbage, shredded	225 g	8 oz	½ lb
Salt and pepper			
Water	450 ml	¾ pt	2 cups

Cut the steak into cubes. Arrange layers of meat, onions, potatoes and cabbage in a pie dish, seasoning well with salt and pepper. Pour in the water. Cover with a piece of foil and cook at 190°C/375°F/ gas mark 5 for 1½ hours. Remove the foil and cover the dish with pastry rolled to fit. Brush with beaten egg. Make a hole in centre and bake at 200°C/400°F/gas mark 6 for 25 minutes.

Lamb and Mushroom Pie

*	*Metric*	*Imperial*	*American*
Shortcrust pastry	*225 g*	*8 oz*	*½ lb*
Shoulder lamb	*450 g*	*1 lb*	*1 lb*
Lambs' kidneys	*2*	*2*	*2*
Seasoned flour	*15 ml*	*1 tbsp*	*1 tbsp*
Oil	*30 ml*	*2 tbsp*	*2 tbsp*
Medium onion, chopped	*1*	*1*	*1*
Stock	*300 ml*	*½ pt*	*1¼ cups*
Mushrooms, halved	*100 g*	*4 oz*	*¼ lb*
Fresh rosemary	*1 sprig*	*1 sprig*	*1 sprig*
Salt and pepper			
Beaten egg to glaze			

Cut the meat into cubes and cut up kidneys, discarding cores. Toss in the seasoned flour. Heat oil and fry the chopped onion until golden. Stir in the lamb and kidney pieces and cook until lightly browned. Stir in the stock, mushrooms and rosemary. Bring to the boil, reduce heat, cover and then simmer for 1 hour until the meat is tender. Season with salt and pepper, remove herbs and turn into a pie dish. Cover with the pastry and brush with beaten egg to glaze. Bake at 200°C/400°F/gas mark 6 for 30 minutes.

Jellied Chicken Pie

	Metric	*Imperial*	*American*
Small chicken	*1*	*1*	*1*
Rashers (slices) streaky bacon, chopped	*3*	*3*	*3*
Carrots. chopped	*2*	*2*	*2*
Onion, chopped	*1*	*1*	*1*
Bayleaf	*1*	*1*	*1*
Water	*1.2 litres*	*2 pts*	*5 cups*
Salt and pepper			
Packet sage and onion stuffing mix	*1*	*1*	*1*
Shortcrust pastry	*225 g*	*8 oz*	*½ lb*
Beaten egg to glaze			
Powdered gelatine	*10 ml*	*2 tsp*	*2 tsp*

Cut chicken in pieces and place in a large pan with the bacon, carrots, onion, bayleaf and water. Season lightly, bring to the boil, cover and simmer gently for 40 minutes until chicken is tender. Take meat out of the pan, remove the bones, and discard skin. Return bones to stock, bring to the boil and simmer for 1 hour. Strain.

Make up stuffing as directed on packet and shape into small balls. Put half the roughly chopped chicken and bacon in a pie dish. Top with stuffing balls then remaining meat. Roll out pasty. Cut a strip and press onto dampened edge of dish. Brush with a little beaten egg then top with pastry. Knock up and flute with the back of a knife. Make a hole in the centre. Cut leaves out of trimmings, arrange around hole. Brush with beaten egg to glaze. Bake at 200°C/400°F/ gas mark 6 for 45 minutes until golden brown.

Dissolve gelatine in 600 ml/1 pt/2 ½ cups of stock. Using a foil funnel, pour liquid into pie through hole in pastry. Leave until cold then chill before serving.

Gillyburn Chicken Pie

*	*Metric*	*Imperial*	*American*
Shortcrust pastry	*350 g*	*12 oz*	*¾ lb*
Pork or beef sausagemeat	*225 g*	*8 oz*	*½ lb*
Large pinch of mixed dried herbs			
Cooked chicken	*350 g*	*12 oz*	*¾ lb*
Plain (all-purpose) flour	*25 g*	*1 oz*	*2 tbsp*
Chicken stock	*300 ml*	*½ pt*	*1¼ cups*
Salt, pepper and sage			
Beaten egg to glaze			

Mix sausagemeat with the herbs and with floured hands, shape into eight balls. Deep-fry sausages until golden brown. Place in a pie dish with the chopped chicken. Stir the flour into fat in pan. Blend in the stock and bring to the boil, stirring well and season if necessary and add sage. Pour into the pie dish and allow to cool. Roll out the pastry and cover the pie dish. Brush with beaten egg, make a hole in the centre and bake at 190°C/ 375°F/gas mark 5 for 30 minutes.

Pork and Kidney Pie

*	Metric	Imperial	American
Shortcrust pastry	225 g	8 oz	½ lb
Pork shoulder	450 g	1 lb	1 lb
Pigs' kidneys	3	3	3
Mixed herbs	10 ml	2 tsp	2 tsp
Stock	300 ml	½ pt	1¼ cups
Dijon mustard	10 ml	2 tsp	2 tsp
Pinch of grated nutmeg			
Medium onion, finely chopped	1	1	1
Medium carrots, finely chopped	2	2	2
Milk or beaten egg to glaze			

Chop the pork and kidneys into small pieces and put into a pie dish with the herbs, stock, mustard, nutmeg, onion and carrots. Cover with a piece of foil and cook at 160°C/325°F/gas mark 3 for 1 hour. Remove the foil and cover the dish with a pastry lid. Brush with milk or beaten egg to glaze. Make a hole in centre. Bake at 200°C/400°F/gas mark 6 for 30 minutes until golden brown.

Turkey Pie

*	Metric	Imperial	American
Puff pastry	*350 g*	*12 oz*	*¾ lb*
Cooked turkey	*350 g*	*12 oz*	*¾ lb*
Hard-boiled (hard-cooked) eggs	*2*	*2*	*2*
Butter	*25 g*	*1 oz*	*2 tbsp*
Plain (all-purpose) flour	*25 g*	*1 oz*	*2 tbsp*
Milk	*150 ml*	*¼ pt*	*⅔ cup*
Turkey stock	*150 ml*	*¼ pt*	*⅔ cup*
Grated rind and juice of lemon	*½*	*½*	*½*
Salt and pepper			
Beaten egg to glaze	*1*	*1*	*1*

Place the diced turkey and quartered hard-boiled eggs in a pie dish. Make a sauce with the butter, flour, milk and stock; bring to the boil, stirring. Add lemon and season well. Pour over the turkey. Roll out the pastry and cover the pie dish. Brush with beaten egg, make a hole in the centre and bake at 220°C/425°F/gas mark 7 for 30 minutes.

Chicken and Leek Pie

	Metric	*Imperial*	*American*
Puff pastry	*350 g*	*12 oz*	*¾ lb*
Chicken	*1.5 kg*	*3 lb*	*3 lb*
Cold water	*1.75 litres*	*3 pts*	*7 ½ cups*
Large onion	*1*	*1*	*1*
Bay leaves	*2*	*2*	*2*
Few parsley stalks			
Salt and pepper			
Medium leeks washed, trimmed and chopped,	*6*	*6*	*6*
Beaten egg to glaze	*1*	*1*	*1*
Double (heavy) cream, warmed	*45 ml*	*3 tbsp*	*3 tbsp*

Place chicken, water, onion, bay leaves and parsley stalks in a large saucepan. Season well, and bring to the boil. Cover and simmer gently for about 1¼ hours or until chicken is tender. Add leeks for last 15 minutes only, then remove them with a draining spoon. Transfer chicken to a plate and allow to cool slightly. Reserve stock. Remove skin from chicken, then cut meat away from the bones. Discard skin and bones, and cut meat into 2.5 cm/1 in pieces. Arrange chicken in the bottom of a 1.5 – 1.75 litre/2½ – 3 pt/6 – 7 ½ cup pie dish and place a pie funnel in the centre. Arrange leeks over chicken. Pour 300 ml/½ pt/ 1¼ cups reserved stock into the dish. Cover with pastry knock up and pinch decoratively. Make a small hole in the centre. Use pastry trimmings to make leaves or a tassel, and arrange around centre of pie. Brush with beaten egg, and bake at 200°C/400°F/gas mark 6 for 40 minutes, until risen and golden. Pour cream into the pie through the centre and serve hot.

Chicken and Potato Pie

	Metric	Imperial	American
Puff pastry	*350 g*	*12 oz*	*¾ lb*
Cooked chicken	*450 g*	*1 lb*	*1 lb*
Potatoes	*450 g*	*1 lb*	*1 lb*
Chicken stock	*300 ml*	*½ pt*	*1¼ cups*
Evaporated milk	*300 ml*	*½ pt*	*1¼ cups*
Chopped fresh parsley	*15 ml*	*1 tbsp*	*1 tbsp*
Salt and pepper			
Beaten egg to glaze			

Cut the chicken and the peeled potatoes into small cubes. Make a rich chicken stock by simmering the carcass in water with plenty of herbs. Mix the stock and the evaporated milk and pour over the chicken and potato in a pie dish. Season well with salt and pepper, and stir in the parsley. Cover with pastry. Brush with beaten egg and make a hole in centre. Bake at 220°C/425°F/gas mark 7 for 40 minutes.

Country Rabbit Pie

*	Metric	Imperial	American
Shortcrust pastry	350 g	12 oz	3/4 lb
Large rabbit	1	1	1
Chopped parsley	15 ml	1 tbsp	1 tbsp
Small onion, finely chopped	1	1	1
Fat bacon, diced	350 g	12 oz	3/4 lb
Plain (all-pupose) flour			
Stock	150 ml	1/4 pt	2/3 cup
Port	30 ml	2 tbsp	2 tbsp
Salt and pepper			
Beaten egg or milk to glaze			

Joint the rabbit and leave it to soak in cold salted water for 6 hours. Drain the joints and wipe dry. Put in a pie dish. Season with salt and pepper, chopped parsley and finely chopped onion. Add the bacon and a light sprinkling of flour. Pour in the stock and port. Cover with pastry, brush with beaten egg or milk and make a hole in centre. Bake at 190°C/375°F/gas mark 5 for 1¼ hours, covering the pastry with a piece of foil if over-browning.

Party Chicken Pie

	Metric	Imperial	American
Puff pastry	225 g	8 oz	½ lb
Beaten egg to glaze			
Butter	75 g	3 oz	⅜ cup
Plain (all-purpose) flour	75 g	3 oz	¾ cup
Chicken stock	600 ml	1 pt	2½ cups
Milk	150 ml	¼ pt	⅔ cup
Cooked chicken, sliced	350 g	12 oz	¾ lb
Mushrooms	225 g	8 oz	½ lb
Sticks of celery, chopped	2	2	2
Toasted blanched almonds	50 g	2 oz	½ cup
Sherry or lemon juice	45 ml	3 tbsp	3 tbsp
Salt and pepper			
Pinch of grated nutmeg			

Roll out pastry and trim to 18 cm/7 in round or large enough to fit the top of a casserole dish. Place on baking sheet. Cut into six triangles, brush with beaten egg and decorate each piece with a pastry leaf.

Whisk butter, flour, stock and milk in a pan. Bring to the boil and cook for 2 minutes stirring until thickened. Add remaining ingredients. Cover and cook very gently for 15 minutes. Bake pastry at 230°C/450°F/gas mark 8 for 10 – 12 minutes. Turn hot chicken mixture into warmed casserole dish and arrange hot pastry triangles on top to serve.

Pigeon Pie

*	*Metric*	*Imperial*	*American*
Shortcrust pastry	*225 g*	*8 oz*	*½ lb*
Streaky bacon rashers (slices)	*6*	*6*	*6*
Medium onions, chopped	*2*	*2*	*2*
Pigeons, quatered	*2*	*2*	*2*
Hard-boiled eggs	*2*	*2*	*2*
Salt and pepper			
Chopped fresh parsley	*15 ml*	*1 tbsp*	*1 tbsp*
Chicken stock	*150 ml*	*¼ pt*	*⅔ cup*
Beaten egg to glaze			

Line a 900 ml/1½ pt/3¾ cup pie dish with the bacon rashers. Sprinkle chopped onion over the top. Place pie funnel in the centre and arrange pigeon pieces and quatered eggs around it. Add seasoning, parsley and stock. Roll out pastry and use to cover pie, cutting out a hole over the funnel. Decorate with leaves made from pastry trimmings. Brush with beaten egg and bake at 180°C/350°F/gas mark 4 for 1½ hours. Lightly cover pastry with foil when golden brown to prevent overbrowning.

Warming Winter Pie

	Metric	*Imperial*	*American*
Shortcrust pastry	*350 g*	*12 oz*	*¾ lb*
Butter or margarine	*50 g*	*2 oz*	*¼ cup*
Leeks, sliced	*225 g*	*8 oz*	*½ lb*
Carrots, chopped	*225 g*	*8 oz*	*½ lb*
Celery, chopped	*225 g*	*8 oz*	*½ lb*
Parsnips, chopped	*225 g*	*8 oz*	*½ lb*
White sauce	*300 ml*	*½ pt*	*1¼ cups*
Cooked bacon or ham	*225 g*	*8 oz*	*½ lb*
Salt and pepper			

Melt butter in a pan, add prepared vegetables and fry gently for 5 minutes. Add 150 ml/¼ pt/⅔ cup water and a little salt and simmer vegetables for 20 minutes; then drain. Combine with white sauce and chopped bacon or ham. Season to taste. Place in a 1.2 litre/2 pt/5 cup pie dish. Leave to cool.

Roll out pastry and cover top of pie. Flute the edges. Decorate top with leaves cut from pastry trimmings and make a hole in the centre. Glaze with a little milk or beaten egg. Bake at 200°C/400°F/gas mark 6 for 25 – 30 minutes.

Fidget Pie

	Metric	*Imperial*	*American*
Shortcrust pastry	*225 g*	*8 oz*	*½ lb*
Lean back bacon	*350 g*	*12 oz*	*¾ lb*
Potatoes, sliced	*450 g*	*1 lb*	*1 lb*
Cooking apples, sliced	*450 g*	*1 lb*	*1 lb*
Salt and pepper			
Chicken stock (or half stock half cider)	*150 ml*	*¼ pt*	*⅔ cup*
Beaten egg to glaze			

Cut each bacon rasher (slice) into three pieces. Arrange layers of sliced potatoes, bacon and sliced apples in a 1.5 litre/2½ pt/6 cup pie dish, until all ingredients are used, seasoning well between each layer. Pour chicken stock into the pie dish.

Cover with pastry. Make a hole in centre. Use trimmings to make pastry leaves, if liked. Brush with beaten egg and bake at 200°C/400°F/gas mark 6 for 20 minutes, then reduce to 180°C/350°F/gas mark 4 and continue to cook for a further 45 minutes.

PLATE PIES AND SAVOURY ROLLS

Plate pies are useful both hot and cold, and slices of them are ideal for packed lunches. These pies with a top and bottom crust may be made in china flan dishes, sponge sandwich tins or flat metal or ovenglass plates. For freezing, they are best made in shallow foil dishes in which they can be frozen and reheated if necessary. Sometimes, the bottom crust of savoury pies becomes soggy, but if the pastry is brushed with a little egg white before the filling is put in, the bottom pastry will remain crisp. A metal container is also much better at conducting heat than a china one and crisper pastry will be the result. It is also a good idea to put a metal baking sheet on the oven shelf while the oven is heating, and the plate pie can then be put on to this hot surface which will also help to make the pastry cook better and be crisper.

Another traditional way of preparing pies is to enclose the filling in a single sheet of pastry, so that a savoury roll is formed which can be conveniently cut into slices. This is a delicious way of making a 'pie' and it can be cooked directly on the baking sheet. Shortcrust, puff or filo pastry may be used for savoury rolls and plate pies.

Savoury Beef Roll

*	Metric	Imperial	American
Shortcrust pastry	*225 g*	*8 oz*	*½ lb*
Raw minced (ground) beef	*450 g*	*1 lb*	*1 lb*
Breadcrumbs, fresh	*75 g*	*3 oz*	*1 ½ cup*
Onion, finely chopped	*1*	*1*	*1*
Ground ginger	*1.5 ml*	*¼ tsp*	*¼ tsp*
Dried mixed herbs	*2.5 ml*	*½ tsp*	*½ tsp*
Salt and pepper			
Beaten egg or milk to glaze			

Put minced beef into a basin, add breadcrumbs, onion, spice and herbs and season to taste. Mix thoroughly with the hand, then form into roll. Place in a well-greased tin, cover well with greased greaseproof (waxed) paper or foil and bake at 190°C/375°F/Gas Mark 5 for 20 minutes.

Put pastry on a floured board and roll into an oblong. Take the roll out of the oven and remove paper. Wrap meat quickly in the pastry. Place on a baking sheet. Put a few pastry leaves on top, brush over with milk or beaten egg and return to the oven. Cook for 30 minutes until the pastry is brown and thoroughly cooked. Serve hot with brown or tomato sauce.

Piquant Corned Beef Pie

*	*Metric*	*Imperial*	*American*
Shortcrust pastry	*225 g*	*8 oz*	*½ lb*
Tins of corned beef	*2 x 350 g*	*2 x 12 oz*	*2 x 12 oz*
Onion, chopped	*175 g*	*6 oz*	*1 –1½ cups*
Oil	*15 ml*	*1 tbsp*	*1 tbsp*
Salt and pepper			
Tabasco pepper sauce	*5 ml*	*1 tsp*	*1 tsp*
Egg	*1*	*1*	*1*
Diced carrots, cooked	*100 g*	*4 oz*	*¼ lb*
Peas	*100 g*	*4 oz*	*¼ lb*
Beaten egg or milk to glaze			

Divide the pastry in half, roll out and line a 20 cm/8 in pie dish. Make up the corned beef filling by mashing up the meat in a basin. Fry the chopped onion in the oil until soft and transparent. Mix into the corned beef with the salt, pepper, Tabasco, egg and finally the diced carrots and the peas. When thoroughly mixed, turn on to the pastry-lined pie dish. Roll out remaining half of pastry. Dampen the pastry rim and seal on the top lid. Flute the pie edge and decorate with pastry 'leaves'. Make a hole in centre. Brush with beaten egg or milk to glaze. Bake at 200°C/400°F/gas mark 6 for 30 minutes. Serve hot or cold.

Chilli Beef Pie

*	Metric	Imperial	American
Shortcrust pastry	350 g	12 oz	¾ lb
Onion, chopped	1	1	1
Raw minced (ground) beef	225 g	8 oz	½ lb
Can red kidney beans	425 g	15 oz	15 oz
Plain (all-purpose) flour	15 ml	1 tbsp	1 tbsp
Water	150 ml	¼ pt	⅔ cup
Pinch of dried oregano			
Salt and pepper			
Chilli powder	1.5 ml	¼ tsp	¼ tsp
Ground cummin	2.5 ml	½ tsp	½ tsp
Tomato purée (paste)	30 ml	2 tbsp	2 tbsp
Beaten egg to glaze			

Fry onion and minced beef until it is brown, stirring. Stir in the flour, water, herbs, tomato purée and seasonings. Cook until the mixture is thick and well blended, stir in the beans. Roll out the pastry into two circles and line a 20 cm/8 in pie plate. Put in the filling and cover with pastry. Glaze and bake at 200°C/400°F/gas mark 6 for 30 minutes. Serve hot or cold.

Summer Lamb Pie

*	Metric	Imperial	American
Puff pastry	*350 g*	*12 oz*	*¾ lb*
Shoulder lamb	*450 g*	*1 lb*	*1 lb*
Medium onion, finely chopped	*1*	*1*	*1*
Oil	*15 ml*	*1 tbsp*	*1 tbsp*
Orange	*1*	*1*	*1*
Grated orange rind	*2.5 ml*	*½ tsp*	*½ tsp*
Lamb stock	*300 ml*	*½ pt*	*1¼ cups*
Cornflour (cornstarch)	*10 ml*	*2 tsp*	*2 tsp*
Salt and pepper			
Dried mint	*2.5 ml*	*½ tsp*	*½ tsp*
Shelled peas	*100 g*	*4 oz*	*¼ lb*
Beaten egg to glaze			

Roll out the pastry and use half to line a pie plate. Chop the lamb in small pieces discarding fat and mix with the onion. Fry in the oil until the onion is soft. Add the juice and rind of the orange with the stock. Simmer for 30 minutes and stir in the cornflour mixed with a little water. Stir in the mint and peas and cool the mixture. Put into the pastry case and cover with the remaining pastry. Knock up and crimp edge. Make a hole in centre. Brush with a little beaten egg to glaze. Bake at 220°C/425°F/gas mark 7 for 40 minutes. Serve hot or cold.

Chopped Pork Pie

*	Metric	Imperial	American
Puff pastry	*350 g*	*12 oz*	*¾ lb*
Belly of pork	*450 g*	*1 lb*	*1 lb*
Dried basil	*5 ml*	*1 tsp*	*1 tsp*
Salt and pepper			
Egg, beaten	*1*	*1*	*1*
Apple sauce	*45 ml*	*3 tbsp*	*3 tbsp*

Roll pastry to oblong 25 cm/10 in long. Mince (grind) or finely chop pork, mix with basil, a little salt and pepper and half the beaten egg. Form into 10 cm/4 in wide roll. Spoon apple down centre of pastry. Top with meat roll. Brush edges of pastry with beaten egg and fold pastry over filling. Place on a baking sheet, keeping the centre join underneath. Glaze with remaining egg and bake at 220°C/425°F/gas mark 7 for 40 minutes. Serve hot or cold.

Roman Pie

*	Metric	Imperial	American
Shortcrust pastry	350 g	12 oz	¾ lb
Vermicelli	50 g	2 oz	⅛ lb
Veal or lean lamb	450 g	1 lb	1 lb
Cooked ham	100 g	4 oz	¼ lb
Grated lemon rind	1.5 ml	¼ tsp	¼ tsp
Salt and pepper			
Pinch of grated nutmeg			
White sauce	150 ml	¼ pt	⅔ cup
Beaten egg to glaze			

Roll out the pastry and use half to line a pie plate. Put the vermicelli into a pan of boiling salted water and boil for 5 – 8 minutes until tender. Drain very thoroughly. Put the vermicelli into the pastry case, pressing it round the bottom and sides so that it lines the pastry. Cut the meat into small cubes and put into the pastry case. Sprinkle on the lemon rind, salt, pepper and nutmeg. Cover with the sauce and top with remaining pastry. Make a hole in centre. Brush with beaten egg to glaze. Bake at 190°C/375°F/ gas mark 5 for 45 minutes – 1 hour. Cover with foil if overbrowning. Serve hot.

Cheshire Pork Pie

*	*Metric*	*Imperial*	*American*
Puff pastry	*450 g*	*1 lb*	*1 lb*
Pork fillet	*900 g*	*2 lb*	*2 lb*
Salt and pepper			
Pinch of grated nutmeg			
Eating apples	*6*	*6*	*6*
Sugar	*50 g*	*2 oz*	*¼ cup*
Dry white wine	*300 ml*	*½ pt*	*1¼ cups*
Butter	*75 g*	*3 oz*	*⅜ cup*
Beaten egg to glaze			

Roll out the pastry into two circles to fit a 25 cm/10 in pie plate. Cut the pork into thin slices and season with salt, pepper and nutmeg. Line the dish with one piece of pastry. Put in a layer of pork, then of peeled and sliced apples and sugar. Top with the remaining pork and add the wine and flakes of butter. Cover with the remaining pastry, cut a hole in the top. Brush with beaten egg. Bake at 220°C/425°F/gas mark 7 for 15 minutes, then reduce heat to 190°C/375°F/gas mark 5 and continue baking for a further 45 minutes. Serve hot or cold.

Veal and Ham Pie

*	*Metric*	*Imperial*	*American*
Shortcrust pastry	*350 g*	*12 oz*	*¾ lb*
Pie veal	*450 g*	*1 lb*	*1 lb*
Bacon	*100 g*	*4 oz*	*¼ lb*
Lemon juice	*10 ml*	*2 tsp*	*2 tsp*
Pinch of dried thyme			
Stock or water	*150 ml*	*¼ pt*	*⅔ cup*
Salt and pepper			
Hard-boiled (hard-cooked) egg	*1*	*1*	*1*
Beaten egg to glaze			

Cut the veal into small dice and the bacon into strips. Season with lemon juice and thyme, add stock or water, and season with salt and pepper. Mix thoroughly and put into a 23 cm/9 in plate. Cut the hard-boiled egg into eight sections and arrange on the meat, white sides uppermost.

Cover with pastry and make a hole in the centre. Knock up and brush with beaten egg to glaze. Decorate with pastry leaves and brush them with egg. Bake at 190°C/375°F/gas mark 5 for 30 minutes, and then at 180°C/350°F/gas mark 4 for 30 minutes. Serve hot or cold.

Chicken or Turkey Tarragon Pie

*	*Metric*	*Imperial*	*American*
Shortcrust pastry	*350 g*	*12 oz*	*¾ lb*
Eggs	*2*	*2*	*2*
Milk	*150 ml*	*¼ pt*	*⅔ cup*
Chopped fresh tarragon	*5 ml*	*1 tsp*	*1 tsp*
Grated rind of lemon	*½*	*½*	*½*
Salt and pepper			
Cooked chicken or turkey meat	*450 g*	*1 lb*	*1 lb*
Beaten egg or milk to glaze			

Blend together eggs and milk. Add tarragon, lemon rind, salt, pepper and chicken or turkey cut into chunky pieces. Reserve one-third of pastry. Roll out remainder into a 23 cm/9 in circle and use to line 18 cm/7 in sandwich tin, leaving 5 mm/¼ in overlap. Fill with chicken mixture and dampen edges.

Roll out remaining pastry to an 20 cm/8 in circle and cover pie. Seal edges, trim and flute. Make six equally spaced radial slits about 2.5 cm/1 in long from centre of pie. Dampen the centre and fold back points making a star. Brush with beaten egg to glaze. Bake at 220°C/425°F/gas mark 7 for 20 minutes. Then at 180°C/350°F/gas mark 4 for a further 40 minutes. Serve hot or cold.

Faggot Pie

*	Metric	Imperial	American
Shortcrust pastry	*350 g*	*12 oz*	*3/4 lb*
Pig's liver	*350 g*	*12 oz*	*3/4 lb*
Lean pork	*450 g*	*1 lb*	*1 lb*
Medium onions, chopped	*2*	*2*	*2*
Oil	*30 ml*	*2 tbsp*	*2 tbsp*
Plain (all-purpose) flour	*30 ml*	*2 tbsp*	*2 tbsp*
Beef stock	*150 ml*	*1/4 pt*	*2/3 cup*
Worcestershire sauce	*30 ml*	*2 tbsp*	*2 tbsp*
Fresh sage	*15 ml*	*1 tbsp*	*1 tbsp*
Salt and pepper			
Milk to glaze			

Mince (grind) liver and pork coarsely. Gently fry the chopped onion in oil until soft, add minced pork and liver and cook, stirring, until brown. Stir in the flour, and add stock, Worcestershire sauce and sage. Cover and cook gently for 30 minutes. Adjust seasoning and cool. Divide the pastry in half and line a 20 cm/8 in pie plate. Add the cooled filling. Use other pastry piece for the lid. Dampen the pastry edges on the plate, cover with the lid, seal, trim, knock up and flute. Roll out the pastry trimmings and cut into thin strips to make a lattice design on top. Brush with milk. Bake at 200°C/400°F/gas mark 6 for 15 minutes. Reduce oven to 180°C/350°F/gas mark 4 and bake for 30 minutes until the pastry is golden and the filling is hot. Serve straight away.

Chicken Jalousie

*	*Metric*	*Imperial*	*American*
Puff pastry	*350 g*	*12 oz*	*¾ lb*
Cooked chicken	*225 g*	*8 oz*	*½ lb*
Can condensed celery soup	*275 ml*	*10 oz*	*10 oz*
Button mushrooms	*50 g*	*2 oz*	*1 cup*
Dried thyme	*5 ml*	*1 tsp*	*1 tsp*
Pinch grated nutmeg			
Beaten egg to glaze			

Roll out the pastry to a rectangle 30 x 20 cm/12 x 8 in. Cut in half across. Roll each piece of pastry to a rectangle 30 x 18 cm/12 x 7in and place one piece on a baking sheet. Fold the other piece in half across its width. Using a sharp knife, make cuts on the folded side to within 2.5 cm/1 in of the cut edges. Open out the pastry, taking care not to stretch it. Mix soup, chicken, mushrooms, thyme and nutmeg together. Pile on to the pastry base, leaving a wide rim all round. Dampen the edges of the pastry with beaten egg; then carefully place the top in position. Knock up edges, brush the top with egg and bake at 220°C/425°F/gas mark 7 for 40 minutes. Serve hot.

Curried Chicken Roll

*	*Metric*	*Imperial*	*American*
Shortcrust pastry	*225 g*	*8 oz*	*½ lb*
Butter	*40 g*	*1½ oz*	*3 tbsp*
Cooked chicken, minced (ground)	*350 g*	*12 oz*	*¾ lb*
Fresh breadcrumbs	*40 g*	*1½ oz*	*¾ cup*
Medium onion, finely chopped	*1*	*1*	*1*
Sultanas (golden raisins)	*25 g*	*1 oz*	*⅙ cup*
Curry powder	*10 ml*	*2 tsp*	*2 tsp*
Salt and pepper			
Egg			
Mango chutney	*30 ml*	*2 tbsp*	*2 tbsp*
Beaten egg to glaze			

Roll out the pastry into a rectangle about 30 x 25 cm/12 x 10 in. Soften the butter and add the minced chicken, breadcrumbs, finely chopped onion and sultanas. Stir in the curry powder, salt, pepper and egg and mix well. Form into a roll about 25 cm/10 in long. Spread mango chutney down centre of pasty. Put the chicken mixture on top and fold pastry over, sealing well. Put on to a baking sheet with the joint underneath. Cut three slits diagonally in the top. Brush with beaten egg to glaze. Bake at 200°C/400°F/Gas Mark 6 for 40 minutes. Serve hot or cold.

Egg and Bacon Pie

*	*Metric*	*Imperial*	*American*
Shortcrust pastry	*350 g*	*12 oz*	*¾ lb*
Streaky bacon	*175 g*	*6 oz*	*⅜ lb*
Chopped fresh parsley	*15 ml*	*1 tbsp*	*1 tbsp*
Eggs	*4*	*4*	*4*
Salt and pepper			
Milk to glaze			

Roll out the pastry to form two rounds to fit an 18 cm/7 in pie plate. Line the plate with one circle of pastry. Cover the base with chopped bacon and parsley. Break in the eggs so they are equally spaced round the plate. Season well with salt and pepper. Cover with remaining pastry and pinch edges together. Make a hole in centre. Brush with a little milk and bake at 200°C/400°F/ gas mark 6 for 30 minutes. Serve hot or cold.

Kentish Bacon Pie

*	Metric	Imperial	American
Puff pastry	*350 g*	*12 oz*	*¾ lb*
Cold boiled bacon	*350 g*	*12 oz*	*¾ lb*
Cherries	*100 g*	*4 oz*	*¼ lb*
White sauce	*150 ml*	*¼ pt*	*⅔ cup*
Mint jelly	*5 ml*	*1 tsp*	*1 tsp*
Pepper			
Beaten egg to glaze			

Line a pie plate with two-thirds of the pastry. Mince the bacon. Stone and quarter the cherries. Mix together the bacon, sauce, mint jelly, pepper and cherries, and fill the pastry case. Make a lid with the remaining pastry. Seal the edges, make a hole in the top and brush pastry with the beaten egg to glaze. Bake at 220°C/425°F/gas mark 7 for 15 minutes, then at 190°C/375°F/gas mark 5 for 20 minutes, or until cooked through. Serve hot or cold.

Bacon and Potato Pasty

*	*Metric*	*Imperial*	*American*
Shortcrust pastry	*225 g*	*8 oz*	*½ lb*
Lean bacon, chopped	*100 g*	*4 oz*	*¼ lb*
Large onion, chopped	*1*	*1*	*1*
Cooked mashed potatoes	*100 g*	*4 oz*	*½ cup*
Cheddar cheese, grated	*50 g*	*2 oz*	*½ cup*
Chopped fresh parsley	*15 ml*	*1 tbsp*	*1 tbsp*
Salt and pepper			
Beaten egg or milk to glaze			

Roll the pastry out to a 20 cm/8 in circle. Mix bacon and onion with the potatoes and cheese. Stir in the parsley, salt and pepper. Put this filling on the pastry. Dampen the edges with a little water and bring up over the filling, pinching the edges to make a large pasty. Transfer to a baking sheet. Brush with beaten egg or milk to glaze. Bake at 190°C/375°F/gas mark 5 for 40 minutes. Serve hot or cold.

Sausage Plait

*	Metric	Imperial	American
Shortcrust pastry	350 g	12 oz	¾ lb
French mustard	15 ml	1 tbsp	1 tbsp
Sausagemeat	450 g	1 lb	1 lb
Small onion, chopped	1	1	1
Dried mixed, herbs	5 ml	1 tsp	1 tsp
Hard-boiled (hard-cooked) eggs	2	2	2
Beaten egg to glaze			

Roll out the pastry to a 30 cm/12 in square. Spread mustard on the pastry. Mix together sausagemeat, onion and herbs and place half of this mixture down the centre third of the pastry, leaving 1 cm/½ in clear at top and bottom. Arrange the sliced hard-boiled eggs on top of sausagemeat, then cover with remaining meat.

Cut in from the edges to within 1 cm/½ in of the filling at 2.5 cm/1 in intervals on both sides of the filling. Brush edges of the pastry with beaten egg. Fold in the 1 cm/½ in pastry at top and bottom and fold alternate strips of pastry from the sides over the filling to form plait, and to cover the filling. Place on a baking sheet. Brush the plait with beaten egg. Bake at 200°C/400°F/gas mark 6 for 20 minutes, then reduce to 180°C/350°F/gas mark 4 and continue cooking for a further 20 minutes. Serve hot or cold.

Terrine en Croute

*	*Metric*	*Imperial*	*American*
Puff pastry	*450 g*	*1 lb*	*1 lb*
Belly pork	*750 g*	*1½ lb*	*1½ lb*
Lean veal	*450 g*	*1 lb*	*1 lb*
Pig's liver	*225 g*	*8 oz*	*½ lb*
Medium onion	*1*	*1*	*1*
Few juniper berries			
Sprig of parsley			
Garlic clove, crushed	*1*	*1*	*1*
Pinch of ground mace			
Salt and pepper			
Madeira	*45 ml*	*3 tbsp*	*3 tbsp*
Dry white wine	*150 ml*	*¼ pt*	*⅔ cup*
Beaten egg to glaze			

Line a 1.2 litre/2 pt/5 cup loaf tin with greased foil. Coarsely mince (grind) meats, onion, juniper berries and parsley. Add the remaining ingredients, except egg, and leave to stand 1 hour. Press mixture firmly into the lined tin then cover with foil. Set in a pan of hot water and bake at 180°C/350°F/gas mark 4 for 1½ hours.

Remove from tin, and cool completely. Roll pastry to a 38 cm/15 in square. Make leaves. Set pâté in the centre, then wrap to form a parcel, seal edges with beaten egg. Set on a baking sheet seam side down, brush with egg and decorate. Bake at 220°C/425°F/gas mark 7 for 30 minutes or until a good golden colour. Serve cold.

Poacher's Roll

*	Metric	Imperial	American
Puff pastry	*350 g*	*12 oz*	*¾ lb*
Streaky bacon, chopped	*175 g*	*6 oz*	*⅜ lb*
Pork sausagemeat	*450 g*	*1 lb*	*1 lb*
Mushrooms, chopped	*50 g*	*2 oz*	*1 cup*
Small onion, chopped	*1*	*1*	*1*
Chopped sage	*5 ml*	*1 tsp*	*1 tsp*
Salt and pepper			
Beaten egg to glaze			

Roll out the pastry to an oblong 33 x 25 cm/13 x 10 in Mix together all ingredients except egg. Form into a sausage shape and place along the centre of the pastry. Brush the pastry edges with water and roll up, sealing the pastry at both ends to enclose the filling completely. Put the pastry roll with the join downwards on a baking sheet. Decorate the top with any pastry trimmings and make three slashes on the surface. Brush with egg and bake at 220°C/425°F/gas mark 7 for 20 minutes, then at 190°C/375°F/gas mark 5 for 40 minutes. Serve hot or cold.

Monday Surprise

	Metric	*Imperial*	*American*
Plain (all-purpose) flour	*225 g*	*8 oz*	*2 cups*
Pinch of salt			
Margarine	*100 g*	*4 oz*	*½ cup*
Cheddar cheese, grated	*100 g*	*4 oz*	*1 cup*
Cayenne pepper	*1.5 ml*	*¼ tsp*	*¼ tsp*
Cold water			
Filling:			
White sauce or thick gravy	*300 ml*	*½ pt*	*1 ¼ cups*
Dried mixed herbs	*2.5 ml*	*½ tsp*	*½ tsp*
Cold cooked meat, diced	*175 g*	*6 oz*	*⅜ lb*
Cooked vegetables, diced	*175 g*	*6 oz*	*⅜ lb*
Salt and pepper			
Beaten egg to glaze			

Make pastry by rubbing margarine into flour and salt. Add cheese and cayenne. Mix with enough water to form a firm dough. Chill. Mix sauce with herbs, meat and vegetables. Season to taste. Roll out pastry to a large square. Spoon filling in centre and brush edges with beaten egg. Wrap pastry over filling to form a parcel. Transfer sealed side down to a baking sheet. Make a bow out of the trimmings and place on the pie to look like a parcel. Brush with beaten egg and bake at 200°C/400°F/gas mark 6 for about 35 minutes. Cover with foil if over browning. Serve hot.

Minted Cheese and Egg Pie

	Metric	*Imperial*	*American*
Shortcrust pastry	*350 g*	*12 oz*	*¾ lb*
Full or half-fat soft cheese	*200 g*	*7 oz*	*scant cup*
Cheddar cheese, grated	*75 g*	*3 oz*	*¾ cup*
Pinch of grated nutmeg			
Salt and pepper			
Eggs (size 4)	*5*	*5*	*5*
Chopped fresh mint	*15 ml*	*1 tbsp*	*1 tbsp*

Roll out half the pastry and use to line a 20 cm/8 in pie plate. Beat cheeses together with the nutmeg and a little salt and pepper. Spread over pastry. Make 4 'wells' in cheese round edge and one in the middle. Break a whole egg into outer ones. Separate final egg and place yolk in centre. Roll out remaining pastry for a lid. Make a hole in centre of pastry lid. Make leaves out of trimmings. Brush with reserved egg white to glaze and bake at 200°C/400°F/gas mark 6 for 40 minutes, covering with foil if turning too brown. Serve cold.

Russian Fish Pie

	Metric	Imperial	American
White fish fillet	750 g	1 ½ lb	1 ½ lb
Onion, chopped	1	1	1
Button mushrooms, sliced	100 g	4 oz	¼ lb
Butter	15 g	½ oz	1 tbsp
Long-grain rice, cooked	50 g	2 oz	½ cup
Hard-boiled (hard-cooked) eggs	3	3	3
Chopped fresh parsley	45 ml	3 tbsp	3 tbsp
Grated nutmeg	1.5 ml	¼ tsp	¼ tsp
Puff pastry	450 g	1 lb	1 lb
Single (light) cream	45–60 ml	3–4 tbsp	3–4 tbsp
Beaten egg to glaze			

Cut fish into cubes, discarding any skin and bones. Fry onion and mushrooms gently in the butter until soft but not brown. Mix with the rice. Shell and chop eggs and mix with parsley and nutmeg. Roll out pastry and trim to an oblong 40 cm x 30 cm/16 in x 12 in. Roll out trimmings to a smaller oblong. Transfer large piece of pastry to a deepened baking sheet. Lay fish down centre, season then top with rice mixture then egg mixture. Draw pastry up to form a case. Spoon in cream. Brush edges of pastry with beaten egg and cover with smaller oblong. Press together to seal then brush with beaten egg. Bake at 200°C/400°F/gas mark 6 for 30 minutes until golden brown and cooked through. Serve hot or cold

FLANS QUICHES AND GOUGÈRES

Savoury flans, or quiches should be cooked in the same way as plate pies to make the crust crisp. Bake the pastry 'blind', if possible, before putting in the filling, then the liquid won't sink into the crust.

A simple flan may be made with leftover meat, cheese, fish or vegetables in a white or cheese sauce. Savoury egg and cream custard quiches are a delicious alternative. The fillings should be thick and creamy, well seasoned with sea salt, freshly-ground pepper, fresh herbs and spices. Gruyère cheese melts smoothly for cheese flans, but Cheddar cheese is more economical.

Shortcrust pastry is the easiest to handle for flans, although puff pastry may be used but this must be well baked so that it is crisp and not too heavy and greasy, particularly if paired with a rich filling. The pastry case may be baked blind and the filling prepared well in advance of cooking. But it should only be put into the pastry case just before baking.

A gougère made with choux pastry is an impressive alternative to a flan or quiche. Before baking the pastry is spooned around the edge of the dish with the filling in the centre.

Quiche Lorraine

*	Metric	Imperial	American
Shortcrust pastry	*225 g*	*8 oz*	*½ lb*
Small onion, chopped	*1*	*1*	*1*
Butter	*15 g*	*½ oz*	*1 tbsp*
Streaky bacon, chopped	*25 g*	*1 oz*	*2 tbsp*
Egg	*1*	*1*	*1*
Egg yolk	*1*	*1*	*1*
Cheddar or gruyère cheese, grated	*50 g*	*2 oz*	*½ cup*
Creamy milk	*150 ml*	*¼ pt*	*⅔ cup*
Pepper			

Roll out the pastry to line a 20 cm/8 in flan ring. Bake blind at 200°C/400°F/gas mark 6 for 10 minutes. Soften onion in the butter. Add the chopped bacon and cook until the onion is golden. Remove pastry case from the oven and spread the bacon and onion mixture on the bottom. Lightly beat the egg, egg yolk, cheese, milk and a little pepper. Add salt if the bacon is not salty. Pour into the flan case and bake at 190°C/375°F/gas mark 5 for 30 minutes. Serve hot or cold.

Farmhouse Quiche

	Metric	*Imperial*	*American*
Shortcrust pastry	*350 g*	*12 oz*	*3/4 lb*
Ham, minced (ground)	*175 g*	*6 oz*	*3/8 lb*
Cottage cheese	*100 g*	*4 oz*	*1/4 lb*
Eggs	*3*	*3*	*3*
Soured (dairy sour) cream	*150 ml*	*1/4 pt*	*2/3 cup*
Salt and pepper			
Tomatoes, sliced	2	2	2

Line a 20 cm/8 in pie plate with the pastry. Mix the ham and cottage cheese. Beat the eggs into the cream, mix all ingredients well (except tomatoes) and season. Pour into the pie dish arrange tomato slices over and bake at 180°C/350°F/gas mark 4 for 15 minutes then at 200°C/400°F/gas mark 6 for 30 minutes until set. Serve hot or cold.

Chicken Raj

	Metric	*Imperial*	*American*
Shortcrust pastry	*225 g*	*8 oz*	*½ lb*
Small onion, chopped	*1*	*1*	*1*
Eating apple, chopped	*1*	*1*	*1*
Butter	*15 g*	*½ oz*	*1 tbsp*
Curry powder	*15 ml*	*1 tbsp*	*1 tbsp*
Eggs	*2*	*2*	*2*
Milk	*150 ml*	*¼ pt*	*⅔ cup*
Salt			
Peach or curried fruit chutney	*30 ml*	*2 tbsp*	*2 tbsp*
Cooked chicken	*175 g*	*6 oz*	*⅜ lb*

Roll out the pastry and line a 20 cm/8 in flan ring. Blind bake for 10 minutes. Place the onion, apple and butter into a small saucepan and cook gently with a lid on for 5 minutes. Add the curry powder and cook for 1 minute, stirring. Cool. Beat eggs, milk and salt together and stir in the curry mixture. Spread chutney over base of flan. Arrange the diced chicken over and pour on the egg mixture. Bake for 30 minutes at 200°C/ 400°F/gas mark 6. Serve hot or cold.

Bacon and Mushroom Quiche

*	*Metric*	*Imperial*	*American*
Shortcrust pastry	*175 g*	*6 oz*	*3/8 lb*
Back bacon, chopped	*100 g*	*4 oz*	*1/4 lb*
Mushrooms, chopped	*100 g*	*4 oz*	*1/4 lb*
Butter	*25 g*	*1 oz*	*2 tbsp*
Large eggs	*2*	*2*	*2*
Milk	*300 ml*	*1/2 pt*	*1 1/4 cups*
Salt and pepper			
Chives or parsley			

Line a pie plate or flan ring with the pastry. Cook bacon and mushrooms in the butter until the mushrooms are just soft. Put into the pastry case. Beat the eggs with the milk and seasoning (the bacon may be salty enough). Pour into the pastry case and bake at 220°C/425°F/gas mark 7 for 35 minutes. Scatter a few chopped chives or a little parsley on the top. Serve hot or cold.

Chicken Lattice Flan

*	*Metric*	*Imperial*	*American*
Puff pastry	*225 g*	*8 oz*	*½ lb*
Cooked chicken, chopped	*225 g*	*8 oz*	*½ lb*
Sweetcorn	*100 g*	*4 oz*	*¼ lb*
White sauce	*300 ml*	*½ pt*	*1¼ cups*
Grated nutmeg	*1.5 ml*	*¼ tsp*	*¼ tsp*
Salt and pepper			
Chopped fresh parsley	*5 ml*	*1 tsp*	*1 tsp*
Beaten egg to glaze			

Roll out the pastry and line a pie plate. Roll out the trimmings and cut them into 1 cm/½ in strips. Mix chicken and corn with the sauce, nutmeg, salt, pepper and parsley. Put into the pastry case and cover with a lattice of pastry strips. Brush with beaten egg to glaze. Bake at 220°C/425°F/gas mark 7 for 40 minutes.

Corned Beef Flan

*	Metric	Imperial	American
Shortcrust pastry	*350 g*	*12 oz*	*¾ lb*
Bacon rashers (slices)	*2*	*2*	*2*
Tin of corned beef, sliced	*350 g*	*12 oz*	*¾ lb*
Tomatoes, sliced	*2*	*2*	*2*
Eggs	*2*	*2*	*2*
Milk	*175 ml*	*6 fl oz*	*¾ cup*
Pinch of dry mustard			
Worcestershire sauce	*10 ml*	*2 tsp*	*2 tsp*

Roll out pastry and line a 23 cm/9 in flan ring. Bake blind at 200°C/400°F/gas mark 6 for 10 minutes. Remove the rind and chop the bacon rashers. Fry until crisp. Beat eggs with the milk, mustard and worcestershire sauce. Arrange corned beef in flan and top with the bacon and tomatoes. Pour over the egg mixture and bake for 35 minutes until the filling is set.

Kidney and Pepper Quiche

*	Metric	Imperial	American
Shortcrust pastry	*350 g*	*12 oz*	*¾ lb*
Medium onion, chopped	*1*	*1*	*1*
Butter	*25 g*	*1 oz*	*2 tbsp*
Green (bell) pepper, chopped	*1*	*1*	*1*
Lambs' kidneys, chopped	*6*	*6*	*6*
Eggs	*3*	*3*	*3*
Milk	*45 ml*	*3 tbsp*	*3 tbsp*
Salt and pepper			
Dried mixed herbs	*2.5 ml*	*½ tsp*	*½ tsp*

Roll out pastry and line a 20 cm/8 in flan ring. Bake blind at 200°C/400°F/gas mark 6 for 10 minutes. Fry the chopped onion in butter for 3 minutes until soft, but not brown. Add chopped kidneys and green pepper. Cook gently, stirring, for 5 minutes. Remove the pan from the heat. Beat eggs, milk, a little salt and pepper and the herbs together. Spread the filling over the base of the flan, and pour the beaten egg mixture over it. Cook at 180°C/350°F/gas mark 4 for 40 minutes, until filling has set.

Mushroom and Onion Quiche

*	*Metric*	*Imperial*	*American*
Shortcrust pastry	*225 g*	*8 oz*	*½ lb*
Onion, chopped	*1*	*1*	*1*
Mushrooms, sliced	*100 g*	*4 oz*	*¼ lb*
Butter or margarine	*15 g*	*½ oz*	*1 tbsp*
Cheddar cheese, grated	*50 g*	*2 oz*	*½ cup*
Eggs	*2*	*2*	*2*
Milk	*300 ml*	*½ pt*	*1 ¼ cups*
Salt and pepper			

Roll out pastry and use to line a 20 cm/8 in flan dish. Bake blind at 200°C/400°F/gas mark 6 for 10 minutes. Meanwhile fry the onion and mushrooms in the butter for 5 minutes, stirring until softened and lightly browned. Turn into flan case. Cover with cheese. Beat eggs and milk together with a little salt and pepper and pour into flan. Bake at 180°C/350°F/gas mark 4 for about 50 minutes until set and golden brown. Serve warm or cold.

Spring Vegetable Quiche

	Metric	*Imperial*	*American*
Shortcrust pastry	*225 g*	*8 oz*	*½ lb*
New potatoes, diced	*225 g*	*8 oz*	*½ lb*
Carrot, diced	*1*	*1*	*1*
Peas	*50 g*	*2 oz*	*½ cup*
Spring onions (scallions) trimmed and chopped	*6*	*6*	*6*
Egg	*1*	*1*	*1*
Milk	*150 ml*	*¼ pt*	*⅔ cup*
Dried mixed herbs	*2.5 ml*	*½ tsp*	*½ tsp*
Salt and pepper			

Roll out pastry and use to line a 20 cm/8 in flan dish. Bake blind at 200°C/400°F/gas mark 6 for 10 minutes. Meanwhile, cook potatoes and carrots in boiling salted water for 5 minutes, add peas and cook 5 minutes more. Drain. Sprinkle spring onions in flan case. Top with cooked vegetables. Beat egg and milk together with the herbs and a little salt and pepper and pour into flan case. Cook at 180°C/350°F/gas mark 4 for about 50 minutes until set and golden brown. Serve hot or cold.

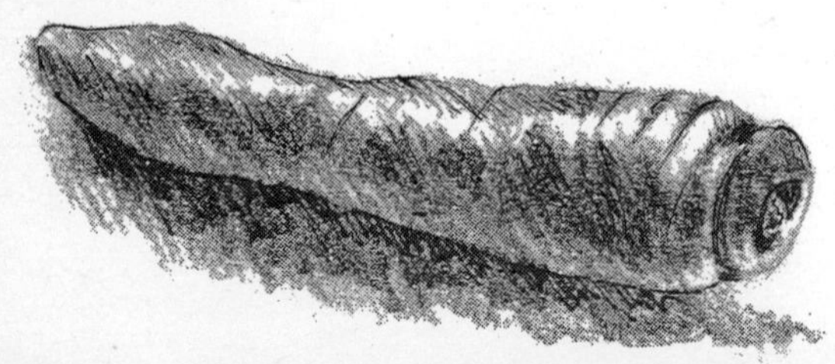

Mediterranean Tomato Flan

*	*Metric*	*Imperial*	*American*
Shortcrust pastry	*225 g*	*8 oz*	*½ lb*
Cinnamon	*5 ml*	*1 tsp*	*1 tsp*
Large onion, chopped	*3*	*3*	*3*
Garlic clove, crushed	*1*	*1*	*1*
Oil	*30 ml*	*2 tbsp*	*2 tbsp*
Can chopped tomatoes	*400 g*	*14 oz*	*14 oz*
Tomato purée (paste)	*15 ml*	*1 tbsp*	*1tbsp*
Pinch of caster (superfine) sugar			
Salt and pepper			
Canned anchovy fillets	*50 g*	*2 oz*	*2 oz*
Black olives	*6*	*6*	*6*
Chopped fresh parsley	*15 ml*	*1 tbsp*	*1 tbsp*

Roll out pastry and use to line a 20 cm/8 in flan dish. Bake blind at 200°C/400°F/gas mark 6 for 10 minutes. Dust all over with cinnamon. Meanwhile fry onion and garlic in the oil for 5 minutes, stirring. Cover with a lid and continue cooking for 10 minutes. Add tomatoes, purée, sugar and a little salt and pepper. Bring to the boil and simmer for 5 – 10 minutes until pulpy. Turn into pastry case, decorate with anchovies and olives and return to oven for 15 minutes. Serve sprinkled with chopped parsley.

Smoked Haddock Quiche

*	Metric	Imperial	American
Shortcrust pastry	*225 g*	*8 oz*	*½ lb*
Smoked haddock	*350 g*	*12 oz*	*¾ lb*
Eggs	*2*	*2*	*2*
Milk	*150 ml*	*¼ pt*	*⅔ cup*
Single (light) cream	*150 ml*	*¼ pt*	*⅔ cup*
Pinch of grated nutmeg			
Chopped fresh parsley	*15 ml*	*1 tbsp*	*1 tbsp*
Salt and pepper			

Roll out pastry and use to line a 20 cm/8 in flan dish. Bake blind at 200°C/400°F/gas mark 6 for 10 minutes. Put the fish in a pan with enough water to cover. Bring to the boil and simmer for 10 minutes until cooked. Drain, flake fish discarding skin and any bones. Turn into cooked flan case.

Beat remaining ingredients together. Pour over fish. Bake at 180°C/350°F/gas mark 4 for about 1 hour until just set. Serve hot or cold.

Parsnip or Sweet Potato Soufflé Pie

	Metric	Imperial	American
Shortcrust pastry	*225 g*	*8 oz*	*½ lb*
Parsnip or sweet potato, cooked	*350 g*	*12 oz*	*¾ lb*
Butter	*25 g*	*1 oz*	*2 tbsp*
Chedder cheese, grated	*50 g*	*2 oz*	*½ cup*
Milk	*60 ml*	*4 tbsp*	*4 tbsp*
Walnut pieces, finely chopped	*100 g*	*4 oz*	*1 cup*
Eggs (size 1), separated	2	2	2
Salt and pepper			
Sweet pickle	*30 ml*	*2 tbsp*	*2 tbsp*

Roll out pastry and use to line a 23 cm/9 in flan dish. Bake blind at 200°C/400°F/gas mark 6 for 10 minutes.

Meanwhile make filling: mash cooked parsnips with the butter, cheese and milk. Stir in nuts and egg yolks. Season well. Whisk egg whites until stiff and fold into mixture with a metal spoon.

Spread pickle over base of flan. Add parsnip filling and bake for 25 minutes until set and golden. Serve hot .

Asparagus Quiche

*	Metric	Imperial	American
Shortcrust pastry	*225 g*	*8 oz*	*½ lb*
Can asparagus tips, drained	*350 g*	*12 oz*	*12 oz*
Gruyère cheese, grated	*75 g*	*3 oz*	*¾ cup*
Eggs, beaten	*2*	*2*	*2*
Single (light) cream	*300 ml*	*½ pt*	*1 ¼ cups*
Salt and pepper			

Roll out pastry and use to line a 20 cm/8 in flan dish. Bake blind at 200°C/400°F/gas mark 6 for 10 minutes. Lay asparagus in flan case. Cover with cheese. Beat eggs and cream together with a little salt and pepper and pour over. Return to oven for about 30 minutes or until golden brown and set. Serve warm or cold.

Spanish Fish Flan

*	Metric	Imperial	American
Shortcrust pastry	*175 g*	*6 oz*	*3/8 lb*
White fish fillet	*225 g*	*8 oz*	*1/2 lb*
milk	*300 ml*	*1/2 pt*	*1 1/4 cups*
Plain (all-purpose) flour	*25 g*	*1 oz*	*1/4 cup*
Butter or margarine	*30 g*	*1 oz*	*2 tbsp*
Tomato purée (paste)	*15 ml*	*1 tbsp*	*1 tbsp*
Canned pimiento, chopped	*1*	*1*	*1*
Salt and pepper			
A few anchovy fillets			
A few stuffed olives			

Roll out pastry and use to line an 18 cm/7 in flan dish. Bake blind at 200°C/400°F/gas mark 6 for 10 minutes. Remove skin and any bones from fish. Cook fish in milk for ten minutes until it flakes easily with a fork. Take fish out of pan. Whisk butter or margarine and flour into milk and bring to the boil, whisking all the time until thickened and smooth. Stir in tomato purée and pimiento. Add flaked fish and season to taste. Pour into flan case, garnish with anchovy fillets and halved olives. Serve warm or cold.

French Spinach Cheese Flan

	Metric	*Imperial*	*American*
Puff pastry	*225 g*	*8 oz*	*½ lb*
Clove garlic, crushed	*1*	*1*	*1*
Small onion, chopped	*1*	*1*	*1*
Oil	*15 ml*	*1 tbsp*	*1 tbsb*
Can chopped tomatoes	*400 g*	*14 oz*	*14 oz*
Tomato purée (paste)	*15 ml*	*1tbsp*	*1tbsp*
Caster (superfine) sugar	*5ml*	*1tsp*	*1tsp*
Salt and pepper			
Spinach, chopped, cooked	*450g*	*1 lb*	*1 lb*
Double (heavy) cream	*30 ml*	*2 tbsp*	*2 tbsp*
Wedge of Saint Paulin or Port Salut Cheese	*175 g*	*6 oz*	*⅜ lb*

Roll out pastry and use to line a 20 cm/8 in flan dish. Prick base well with a fork then bake blind for 10 minutes until risen and golden. If necessary, gently press down centre of cooked case.

Meanwhile fry garlic and onion in the oil for 3 minutes. Add tomatoes, purée, sugar and a little seasoning. Boil rapidly until well reduced – about 8 minutes. Mix well drained cooked spinach with cream. Cut rind off cheese then cut wedge into 6 thin wedges (a wet knife helps!). Put tomato mixture in flan. Spoon spinach mixture over and top with wedges of cheese, in a starburst pattern. Cook in oven at 180°C/350°F/gas mark 4 for about 6 minutes until warmed through and cheese is melting. Serve straight away.

Tangy Cheese and Carrot Flan

	Metric	*Imperial*	*American*
Shortcrust pastry	*225 g*	*8 oz*	*½ lb*
Carrots, sliced	*4*	*4*	*4*
Pure orange juice	*150 ml*	*¼ pt*	*⅔ cup*
Grated rind of orange	*½*	*½*	*½*
Curd or half-fat soft cheese	*225 g*	*8 oz*	*1 cup*
Salt			
Arrowroot	*5 ml*	*1 tsp*	*1tsp*
Orange, segmented	*1*	*1*	*1*

Roll out pastry and use to line a 23 cm/9 in flan dish. Bake blind at 200°C/400°F/gas mark 6 for 10 minutes. Meanwhile cook carrots in orange juice and a little salt until tender. Drain reserving juice. Beat cheese and orange rind together and spread into flan. Cover with carrots, arranged attractively. Blend arrowroot with 2 tsp water. Stir into orange juice and cook until thickened and clear, stirring all the time. Spoon over carrots and decorate with orange segments. Chill until ready to serve.

Cheese and Onion Gougère

*	*Metric*	*Imperial*	*American*
Onion, thinly sliced	*450 g*	*1 lb*	*1 lb*
Butter	*15 g*	*½ oz*	*1 tbsp*
Plain (all-purpose) flour	*25 g*	*1 oz*	*¼ cup*
Milk	*150 ml*	*¼ pt*	*⅔ cup*
Gruyère cheese, grated	*175 g*	*6 oz*	*1 ½ cups*
Salt and pepper			
Choux pastry	*x 2*	*x 2*	*x 2*

Make filling: fry onion gently in butter for 10 minutes until really soft but not brown, stirring occasionally. Add flour and cook for 1 minute. Stir in the milk. Bring to the boil, stirring until thickened. Add 100 g/4 oz/1 cup of the cheese and season to taste. Grease a shallow ovenproof dish and spoon pastry round edge. Spoon onion mixture in centre and sprinkle choux pastry with remaining cheese. Bake at 200°C/400°F/gas mark 6 for about 30 minutes until risen, crisp and golden. Serve hot or cold.

Cod Provençal Gougère

*	Metric	Imperial	American
Onion, chopped	*1*	*1*	*1*
Clove garlic, crushed	*1*	*1*	*1*
Oil	*15 ml*	*1 tbsp*	*1 tbsp*
Can tomatoes	*400 g*	*14 oz*	*14 oz*
Tomato purée (paste)	*15 ml*	*1 tbsp*	*1 tbsp*
Dried mixed herbs	*2.5 ml*	*½ tsp*	*½ tsp*
Salt and pepper			
Cod fillet, skinned and boned	*225 g*	*8 oz*	*½ lb*
Black olives, stoned	*8*	*8*	*8*
Choux pastry	*x 2*	*x 2*	*x 2*

Fry onion and garlic in oil for 3 minutes. Add tomatoes, purée, herbs and a little salt and pepper. Bring to the boil and simmer for 8 minutes until pulpy. Dice fish and add. Spoon choux pastry round edge of a 1.75 litre/3 pt/7 ½ cup shallow ovenproof dish. Spoon fish mixture in centre and sprinkle with olives. Bake at 200°C/400°F/gas mark 6 for about 30 – 35 minutes until pastry is risen, crisp and golden. Serve hot.

Blushing Pilchard Gougère

*	*Metric*	*Imperial*	*American*
Onion, chopped	*1*	*1*	*1*
Butter or margarine	*25 g*	*1 oz*	*2 tbsp*
Plain (all purpose) flour	*25 g*	*1 oz*	*¼ cup*
Fish or vegetable stock	*300 ml*	*½ pt*	*1 ¼ cups*
Small cooked beetroot (beets), diced	*4*	*4*	*4*
Can pilchards in tomato sauce	*200 g*	*7 oz*	*7 oz*
Pepper			
Choux pastry	*x 2*	*x 2*	*x 2*
Parsley to garnish			

Cook onion in the butter or margarine for 3 minutes, stirring. Blend in flour then whisk in the stock and bring to the boil, whisking all the time. Remove from the heat. Add beetroot. Remove bones from pilchards then add fish and sauce to pan. Stir in gently and season with pepper to taste.

Spoon choux pastry round edge of a 1.5 litre/ 2 ½ pt/6 cup shallow ovenproof dish. Spoon filling in centre and bake at 200°C/400°F/gas mark 6 for about 40 minutes until pastry is risen, crisp and golden. Serve hot, garnished with parsley.

Normandy Flan

	Metric	*Imperial*	*American*
Filo pastry sheets	*8*	*8*	*8*
Melted butter			
Frozen chopped spinach, thawed	*225 g*	*8 oz*	*½ lb*
Camembert, sliced	*175 g*	*6 oz*	*⅜ lb*
Eggs	*3*	*3*	*3*
Single (light) cream	*300 ml*	*½ pt*	*1 ¼ cup*
Salt and pepper			
Pinch of grated nutmeg			

Lightly butter a 20 cm/8 in square flan dish. Layer pastry sheets in dish each brushed with a little melted butter, letting pastry hang over edges.

Drain spinach well on kitchen paper then place in pastry-lined dish. Top with sliced cheese. Beat eggs with cream and a little salt, pepper and nutmeg. Pour over then fold pastry over top. Brush lightly with a little more butter and bake at 180°C/350°F/gas mark 4 for 30 – 35 minutes until golden brown and set. Serve warm.

RAISED PIES

These pies were formerly 'raised' by moulding the pastry around wooden moulds, and the pastry formed a thick wall which contained a savoury filling and could be baked without a container. It is possible to use the same technique by moulding the pastry around a jam jar, but most people now prefer to put these pies into hinged pie moulds, or loosed-bottomed cake tins.

The traditional pastry for raised pies is hot water crust. The pastry has to be moulded into thick walls for strength, and also to withstand the long cooking which is necessary to penetrate the dense filling. This pastry absorbs the rich meat juices and fat so that it becomes soft inside but remains crisp outside.

Make up the hot water pastry as indicated in the first chapter: ALL ABOUT PASTRY. The pastry should be mixed well and then rested for 20 minutes before moulding or it will collapse before filling. If it is left until too cold, it will crack and be difficult to handle. If the pie is made in a tin, the sides of the tin can be removed for the last half hour of cooking so that the pastry browns well as this pastry should be richly coloured. Use about three-quarters of the pastry for the case, unless a recipe indicates otherwise and mould it quickly with the hands up the sides of the tin, leaving no cracks. Pack the filling tightly and cover with the pastry lid, sealing the edges firmly. Glaze the pastry by brushing thickly with a beaten egg, to which a pinch of salt has been added.

One of the nicest things about a raised meat pie is the savoury jelly which surrounds the filling. For this, ideally stock should be made from the bones and trimmings of the meat which is used. This needs simmering for 3 – 4 hours so that it will set firmly, and if a pig's trotter or calf's foot can be added, this will increase the firmness of the jelly. When the stock has simmered for 3 – 4 hours, strain it and reduce to about 450 ml/¾ pt/2 cups stock. Season with salt and pepper and cool quickly. However, you can cheat by using 300 ml/½ pt/1¼ cups liquid made with a good quality stock cube and disolving 10 ml/2 tsp of gelatine in it! The stock should not be put into the pie until the pastry is cold and the filling almost firm. The stock should be the consistency of egg white, and should be poured into the pie through a very small funnel (one can easily be made with a piece of foil) and the pie should be left until completely cold and firm before cutting. Other savoury raised pies can be made using shortcrust pastry. Don't make the walls too thin though or your pie will collapse!

Pork Pie

	Metric	*Imperial*	*American*
Hot water pastry	*750 g*	*1½ lb*	*1½ lb*
Shoulder pork, finely diced	*900 g*	*2 lb*	*2 lb*
Chopped fresh sage	*10 ml*	*2 tsp*	*2 tsp*
Salt and pepper			
Pinch of grated nutmeg			
Jellied stock			
Beaten egg to glaze			

Make up the pastry and mould three-quarters of it. Mix meat with the sage, salt, pepper and nutmeg. Fill the case and add 3 tablespoons stock. Cover with remaining pastry, decorate and make a hole in the top. Brush with beaten egg to glaze. Bake at 220°C/425°F/gas mark 7 for 30 minutes, and then at 160°C/325°F/gas mark 3 for 1½ hours, covering the pastry with foil if it is getting too brown. Leave to cool slightly, and then pour in the stock. Leave the pie until cold and firm before cutting.

Economy Pork Pie

	Metric	Imperial	American
Hot water pastry	*750 g*	*1½ lb*	*1½ lb*
Pork pieces	*450 g*	*1 lb*	*1 lb*
Pork sausagemeat	*225 g*	*8 oz*	*½ lb*
Mixed herbs	*1.5 ml*	*¼ tsp*	*¼ tsp*
Pinch of mace			
Bay leaf, chopped	*1*	*1*	*1*
Breadcrumbs	*15 ml*	*1 tbsp*	*1 tbsp*
Salt and pepper			
Hard-boiled (hard-cooked) eggs	*4*	*4*	*4*
Stock or water	*150 ml*	*¼ pt*	*⅔ cup*
Beaten egg to glaze			
Gelatine	*10 ml*	*2 tsp*	*2 tsp*

Make up the pastry and use three-quarters of it to mould the case. Chop or mince (grind) the pork and mix with the sausagemeat, herbs, spices and breadcrumbs. Season well with salt and pepper. Put half the mixture into the pie case and arrange the hard-boiled eggs on top. Fill up with remaining mixture and 1 tbsp stock or water. Cover with the remaining pastry and decorate. Brush with beaten egg to glaze. Bake at 220°C/425°F/gas mark 7 for 30 minutes and then at 160°C/325°F/ gas mark 3 for 1½ hours. Cool slightly and pour in stock with gelatine dissolved in it. Leave until cold and firm before cutting.

Pork and Apple Pies

	Metric	Imperial	American
Hot water pastry	750 g	1½ lb	1½ lb
Lean pork, minced (ground)	450 g	1 lb	1 lb
Large onion, minced (ground)	1	1	1
Cooking (tart) apple, minced (ground)	1	1	1
White wine or cider	30 ml	2 tbsp	2 tbsp
Salt and pepper			
Chopped sage	5 ml	1 tsp	1 tsp
Beaten egg to glaze			
Stock or water	300 ml	½ pt	1¼ cups
Gelatine	10 ml	2 tsp	2 tsp

Mix together the meat, onion, apple, wine, a little salt and pepper and the sage. Divide the pastry into eight pieces. For each piece proceed as follows: Cut off one-third of the pastry for the lid, cover, and put aside. Roll out the remaining pastry to a round approximately 14 cm/5½ in diameter. Dredge a 6 cm/2½ in upturned jar or canister heavily with flour. Lift the pastry on a rolling pin and transfer it to the jar. Shape the pastry by pressing it firmly against the sides. Cut a piece of greaseproof paper or baking parchment long enough to go completely round the pie. Wrap the paper round the pastry; secure with string or a pin. Allow pastry to rest in a cool place until firm. Turn the jar over and ease it out of the pastry case, twisting at first to loosen it. Repeat to make eight pies.

Fill the pie cases with the meat mixture, packing it well at the sides to hold the shape of the pies. Roll out each pie lid, brush the edge of each lid with beaten egg and press this to the upper edge of the pie between finger and thumb. Pinch the edges between finger and thumb all round to flute them. Glaze the tops with beaten egg, using any remaining pastry for decoration. Make holes to let out the steam.

Bake at 200°C/400°F/gas mark 6 for 30 minutes. Remove paper from the sides, cook for a further 30 minutes at 180°C/350°F/gas mark 4. Allow to cool. Make the jelly by placing the stock and gelatine in a saucepan. Stir on a low heat until the gelatine has dissolved, season to taste. Leave until cold and on the point of setting then pour into the pies. Chill before serving.

Veal, Ham and Egg Pie

	Metric	*Imperial*	*American*
Hot water pastry	*450 g*	*1 lb*	*1 lb*
Pie veal, diced small	*450 g*	*1 lb*	*1 lb*
Raw ham or lean bacon, diced small	*100 g*	*4 oz*	*¼ lb*
Dried thyme	*2.5 ml*	*½ tsp*	*½ tsp*
Salt and pepper			
Hard-boiled (hard-cooked) egg	*1*	*1*	*1*
Jellied stock	*300 ml*	*½ pt*	*1¼ cups*

Mould three-quarters of the pastry. Cut the veal and ham into small pieces and mix with the thyme, salt and pepper. Put half the mixture into the pie case and put the egg in the centre. Cover with the remaining meat mixture and add 30 ml/2 tbsp stock. Cover with remaining pastry and decorate. Bake at 220°C/425°F/gas mark 7 for 30 minutes, and then at 160°C/325°F/gas mark 3 for 1½ hours, covering the pastry with foil if it browns too quickly. Leave to cool. Pour in the almost set stock. Chill before cutting.

Jugged Hare Pie

	Metric	*Imperial*	*American*
Hot water pastry	*450 g*	*1 lb*	*1 lb*
Joints of hare, boned	*3*	*3*	*3*
Fresh parsley and thyme	*10 ml*	*2 tsp*	*2 tsp*
Salt and pepper			
Red wine	*45 ml*	*3 tbsp*	*3 tbsp*
Red currant jelly	*30 ml*	*2 tbsp*	*2 tbsp*
Brandy	*15 ml*	*1 tbsp*	*1 tbsp*
Cold jellied stock			
Beaten egg to glaze			

Chop or mince (grind) the hare finely, season with herbs, salt and pepper, and leave to stand overnight in wine, redcurrant jelly and brandy. Make up the pastry and line an 18 cm/7 in loose-bottomed cake tin. Mix the hare with 15 ml/1 tbsp of stock and put into the pastry case. Brush the top edge with beaten egg, and put on the lid. Glaze the lid with beaten egg and make a hole in the centre.

Bake at 200°C/400°F/gas mark 6 for 20 minutes; then reduce heat to 180°C/350°F/gas mark 4 for one hour, covering the pastry to prevent over-browning. Cool the pie and pour in a little cold jellied stock which is almost at setting point. Leave in the tin until completely cold.

Game Pie

	Metric	Imperial	American
Hot water pastry	*750 g*	*1½ lb*	*1½ lb*
Pork sausagemeat	*350 g*	*12 oz*	*¾ lb*
Lean bacon or raw ham	*100 g*	*4 oz*	*¼ lb*
Lean chuck steak	*175 g*	*6 oz*	*⅜ lb*
Pheasant, or any game meat	*1 - 2*	*1 - 2*	*1 - 2*
Salt and pepper			
Ground mace	*2.5 ml*	*½ tsp*	*½ tsp*
Jellied stock	*150 - 300 ml*	*¼ - ½ pt*	*⅔ - 1¼ cups*

Make up the pastry and use three-quarters of it to line a hinged game pie mould or a loose bottomed cake tin, pressing the pastry well into the sides of the tin. Line with a thin layer of sausagemeat. Cut the bacon and steak into small cubes. Strip the flesh from the game and cut it in small pieces discarding skin. Mix the meats well together and season with salt, pepper and the mace. Add about 60 ml/4 tbsp stock and pack the meat into the case. Cover with lid, decorate, make a hole in the centre. Bake at 220°C/425°F/gas mark 7 for 30 minutes; then lower heat to 190°C/375°F/ gas mark 5 for 30 minutes. Reduce heat again to 180°C/350°F/gas mark 4 and bake for 30 minutes more. Cover the pie with foil if it is becoming too brown. Take the pie from the oven, fill up with hot stock and leave to cool. Chill overnight before removing tin.

Chicken and Bacon Raised Pie

	Metric	Imperial	American
Hot water pastry	750 g	1½ lb	1½ lb
Collar bacon, diced	275 g	10 oz	⅝ lb
Boneless chicken, diced	275 g	10 oz	⅝ lb
Chopped fresh parsley	15 ml	1 tbsp	1 tbsp
Grated rind of a small lemon	1	1	1
Salt and pepper			
A little stock or water			
Hard-boiled (hard-cooked) egg	1	1	1
Beaten egg to glaze			
Gelatine	10 ml	2 tsp	2 tsp
Chicken stock	300 ml	½ pt	1¼ cups

Mix together bacon, chicken, parsley, lemon rind, salt and pepper. Moisten with a little stock or water. Knead the pastry for 2 minutes until smooth and free from cracks. Roll out two-thirds of the pastry, and use to line a 15 cm/6 in loose-bottomed round cake tin. Half fill the pastry case with the meat mixture. Put the egg in the centre and add the remaining meat mixture. Roll out lid, cover and decorate pie with pastry trimmings. Glaze the top with a little beaten egg. Bake at 220°C/425°F/gas mark 7 for 15 – 20 minutes. Then at 180°C/350°F/gas mark 4 for a further 1 – 1½ hours, or until meat feels tender when tested with a skewer. Cool. Dissolve the gelatine in stock. When almost set pour into pie and chill.

Picnic Pie

	Metric	Imperial	American
Shortcrust pastry	*450 g*	*1 lb*	*1 lb*
Bunch of spring onions (scallions), chopped	*1*	*1*	*1*
Tomatoes, chopped	*2*	*2*	*2*
Butter	*25 g*	*1 oz*	*2 tbsp*
Corned beef	*350 g*	*12 oz*	*¾ lb*
Sweet pickle	*30 ml*	*2 tbsp*	*2 tbsp*
Long-grain rice, cooked	*100 g*	*4 oz*	*¼ lb*
Salt and pepper			
Hard-boiled (hard-cooked) eggs	*3*	*3*	*3*
A little flour for dusting			
Beaten egg to glaze			

Line a 900 g/2 lb loaf tin with double thickness foil, folding down edges over rim of tin.

Cut off about ¼ of the pastry and reserve for a 'lid'. Roll out remainder and use to line tin, pressing dough gently into corners. Fry onions and tomatoes in the butter for 2 minutes. Mash corned beef. Work in the pickle, rice, onion mixture and a little salt and pepper. Press half the mixture into tin. Dust eggs with flour and lay down centre. Top with remaining mixture and press down well. Roll out remaining pastry for a 'lid'. Brush edges with beaten egg and press 'lid' in position. Crimp between fingers and thumb. Make leaves out of trimmings and place on top. Make a small hole in centre. Brush with beaten egg. Bake at 200°C/400°F/gas mark 6 for 20 minutes then at 180°C/350°F/gas mark 4 for a further 1 hour. Cover with foil if over browning.

Leave to cool in tin for 30 minutes then lift out using foil, place on a rack and gently fold foil down. Leave until cold. Chill until ready to serve.

Farmhouse Vegetable Pie

	Metric	Imperial	American
Medium potatoes, thinly sliced	*2*	*2*	*2*
Large carrot, thinly sliced	*3*	*3*	*3*
Onions, thinly sliced	*2*	*2*	*2*
Peas	*50 g*	*2 oz*	*½ cup*
Chedder cheese, grated	*175 g*	*6 oz*	*1 ½ cups*
Shortcrust pastry	*450 g*	*1 lb*	*1 lb*
Chopped fresh parsley	*15 ml*	*1 tbsp*	*1 tbsp*
Chopped fresh thyme	*15 ml*	*1 tbsp*	*1 tbsp*
Eggs	*2*	*2*	*2*
Milk	*150 ml*	*¼ pt*	*⅔ cup*
Salt and pepper			

Fry vegetables, except peas, in butter for 5 minutes, stirring, until soft but not brown. Leave to cool then stir in peas and cheese. Cut off about ¼ of the dough and reserve for lid. Roll out remainder and use to line an 18 cm/7 in deep, round, loose-bottomed cake tin, easing pastry into corners. Fill with cool vegetable mixture. Keep 15 ml/1 tbsp egg for glazing, beat remainder with milk, parsley and thyme and a little salt and pepper. Pour over. Roll out reserved pastry for lid. Brush edges with a little of the reserved egg and press lid in position. Crimp between finger and thumb. Make leaves out of trimmings. Make a hole in centre. Brush with remaining egg to glaze. Bake at 200°C/400°F/gas mark 6 for about 20 minutes then at 180°C/350°F/ gas mark 4 for a further $1\frac{1}{4}$ hours or until vegetables feel tender when a skewer is inserted right down through centre hole.

Leave to cool in the tin for at least 30 minutes then stand tin on a storage jar, hold firmly and slide side down leaving pie sitting on base. Slide off base using a palette knife, and cool completely on a wire rack.

INDIVIDUAL PIES

Small pies and pastries are always popular because they can be used as snacks and packed meals, or make a main meal with vegetables or salad; they can also be used for parties. They are the ideal way of eking out a small quantity of ingredients, and always look tempting. Shortcrust pastry provides a firmer casing for the filling – best for picnics and packed lunches, but for parties or meals at home, lighter puff or filo pastry may be preferred.

Vegetable Samosas

	Metric	Imperial	American
Pastry			
Self-raising (self-rising) flour	*175 g*	*6 oz*	*1½ cups*
Shredded (chopped) suet	*75 g*	*3 oz*	*¾ cup*
Pinch of salt			
Filling			
Small onion, grated	*1*	*1*	*1*
Curry powder	*5 ml*	*1 tsp*	*1 tsp*
Oil	*15 ml*	*1 tbsp*	*1 tbsp*
Cooked mashed potato	*175 g*	*6 oz*	*¾ cup*
Peas	*50 g*	*2 oz*	*½ cup*
Salt and pepper			
Mango chutney	*15 ml*	*1 tbsp*	*1 tbsp*
Oil for deep frying			

Make up the pastry by mixing the flour, suet and salt with enough cold water to make a firm dough. Roll out and cut into eight rounds. Fry onion and curry powder in the oil for 3 minutes, stirring. Remove from heat. Add the potato, chutney and peas. Season with salt and pepper and cool. Put a spoonful of the mixture in the centre of each pastry round. Dampen edges. Bring up the edges and pinch together to make a pasty shape. Fry in hot oil for about 5 minutes until the pastry is golden. Drain on kitchen paper. Serve hot with chutney.

Salmon Sensations

*	*Metric*	*Imperial*	*American*
Filo pastry sheets	*4*	*4*	*4*
Melted butter			
Salmon cutlets, skinned and bone removed	*4*	*4*	*4*
Garlic and herb cheese	*90 g*	*3 ½ oz*	*scant ½ cup*
Lemon, rind and juice	*1*	*1*	*1*
Mayonnaise	*45 ml*	*3 tbsp*	*3 tbsp*
Tomato purée (paste)	*15 ml*	*1 tbsp*	*1 tbsp*
Worcestershire sauce	*5 ml*	*1 tsp*	*1 tsp*

Lay filo sheets on work surface. Brush lightly with the melted butter and fold in half to form squares. Brush with a little more butter. Put a salmon cutlet in the centre of each. Fill centre where bone has been removed with cheese. Sprinkle with lemon rind and a squeeze of the juice. Draw pastry up over filling and gather together to form parcels. Transfer to a buttered baking sheet. Brush with a little more butter and bake at 190°C/375°F/gas mark 5 for 12 – 15 minutes until golden and cooked through. Meanwhile blend mayonnaise with the purée and worcestershire sauce. Serve with the salmon sensations.

Devon Lamb Pies

*	*Metric*	*Imperial*	*American*
Puff pastry	*350 g*	*12 oz*	*¾ lb*
Cold cooked lamb	*225 g*	*8 oz*	*½ lb*
Cold boiled ham or bacon	*50 g*	*2 oz*	*4 tbsp*
Plain (all-purpose) flour	*5 ml*	*1 tsp*	*1 tsp*
Chopped fresh parsley	*5 ml*	*1 tsp*	*1 tsp*
Dried mint	*2.5 ml*	*½ tsp*	*½ tsp*
Salt and pepper			
Thick brown gravy	*150 ml*	*¼ pt*	*⅔ cup*
Beaten egg or milk to glaze			

Chop the lamb and ham or bacon. Mix with the flour, parsley and mint. Season lightly. Roll out the pastry and cut out twelve rounds. Line six individual patty tins and fill these with the meat mixture. Add gravy to each, put on lids and make a slit in the centre of each. Brush with beaten egg or milk. Bake at 200°C/400°F/gas mark 6 for 30 minutes. Heat any left-over gravy and pour it into the pies before serving, or serve separately.

Lamb Parcels

	Metric	*Imperial*	*American*
Puff pastry	*225 g*	*8 oz*	*½ lb*
Lamb cutlets	*4*	*4*	*4*
Salt and pepper			
Squeeze of lemon juice			
Curry powder	*2.5 ml*	*½ tsp*	*½ tsp*
Eating apples, sliced	*2*	*2*	*2*
Beaten egg to glaze			

Roll the pastry into a square about 5 mm/¼ in thick and cut into four triangles. Season the cutlets with salt, pepper and curry powder, rubbing the seasoning well in. Peel and slice the apples and toss them in lemon juice. Put one lamb cutlet on each triangle of pastry and top with apple slices. Damp the edges of the pastry and form into parcels, leaving the cutlet bones sticking out. Transfer to a baking sheet. Brush the pastry with beaten egg to glaze. Put a twist of foil round each cutlet bone so that they will not burn as the pastry cooks. Bake at 220°C/425°F/ gas mark 7 for 35 minutes. Serve hot.

Cornish Pasties

*	Metric	Imperial	American
Shortcrust pastry	*900 g*	*2 lb*	*2 lb*
Chuck or blade steak, diced small	*225 g*	*8 oz*	*½ lb*
Small onion, finely chopped	*1*	*1*	*1*
Small (white) turnip, diced small	*1*	*1*	*1*
Small carrot, diced small	*1*	*1*	*1*
Medium potato, diced small	*1*	*1*	*1*
Salt and pepper			
Beaten egg to glaze			

Mix meat and vegetables together. Season well. Roll pastry out thinly. Using a small saucepan lid or plate as a guide, cut out twenty four 13 cm/ 5 in circles of pastry. Or fewer larger ones if preferred. Divide filling between pastry rounds, damp edges of pastry, and draw edges together to form a join across the top. Press well together and flute the edges. Place on a baking sheet, brush with beaten egg and bake at 200°C/400°F/gas mark 6 for 15 minutes. Then at 180°C/350°F/gas mark 4 for 35 minutes until the pastry is golden and the filling tender. Serve hot or cold.

Spiced Beef Puffs

*	Metric	Imperial	American
Puff pastry	750 g	1½ lb	1½ lb
Oil	15 ml	1 tbsp	1 tbsp
Butter	15 g	½ oz	1 tbsp
Medium onion, chopped	1	1	1
Raw minced (ground) beef	225 g	8 oz	½ lb
Small green (bell) pepper, chopped	1	1	1
Ground ginger	1.5 ml	¼ tsp	¼ tsp
Chilli(chili) powder	1.5 ml	¼ tsp	¼ tsp
Tomato purée (paste)	15 ml	1 tbsp	1 tbsp
Salt and pepper			
Stuffed olives	6	6	6
Egg, beaten	1	1	1

Heat oil and butter in a pan and fry chopped onion gently until soft. Stir in mince and cook until brown, stirring all the time. Add chopped green pepper, ginger, chilli powder, tomato purée and salt and pepper. Cover and cook gently for 10 minutes. Add stuffed olives and allow mixture to cool. Roll out pastry and cut into eight 15 cm/ 6 in circles and prick with a fork. Place a spoonful of beef mixture in centre of each and dampen edges. Fold in half and seal edges firmly. Chill for 30 minutes. Brush tops with beaten egg and bake at 220°C/425°F/gas mark 7 for 20 minutes until risen and golden. Serve hot or cold.

Little Chicken Pies

*	Metric	Imperial	American
Puff pastry	*350 g*	*12 oz*	*¾ lb*
Small chicken	*1*	*1*	*1*
Mushrooms, sliced	*100 g*	*4 oz*	*2 cups*
Medium onion, finely chopped	*1*	*1*	*1*
Vinegar	*15 ml*	*1 tbsp*	*1 tbsp*
Chopped fresh parsley	*5 ml*	*1 tsp*	*1 tsp*
Salt	*2.5 ml*	*½ tsp*	*½ tsp*
Worcestershire sauce	*2.5 ml*	*½ tsp*	*½ tsp*
Streaky bacon rashers (slices)	*4*	*4*	*4*
Beaten egg to glaze			

Take the raw meat off chicken, discard skin and roughly cut up. Simmer the carcass in just enough water to cover it for an hour to make stock. Mix all ingredients (except stock) together. Put into six individual pie dishes. Half-fill each dish with stock and cover with pastry. Brush the pastry with a little beaten egg, make a hole in each, and bake at 220°C/425°F/gas mark 7 for 15 minutes then at 180°C/350°F/gas mark 4 for 45 minutes. Serve hot.

Sausage Pasties

	Metric	*Imperial*	*American*
Puff pastry	*225 g*	*8 oz*	*½ lb*
Pork sausagemeat	*225 g*	*8 oz*	*½ lb*
Dried sage	*1.5 ml*	*¼ tsp*	*¼ tsp*
Hard-boiled (hard-cooked) eggs	*2*	*2*	*2*
Small onion, grated	*1*	*1*	*1*
Salt and pepper			
Beaten egg to glaze			

Mix sausagemeat, sage, chopped up eggs, onion and seasonings together. Roll out pastry thinly and cut into four 15 cm/6 in circles. Divide filling between pastry rounds, leaving a clear edge all round. Dampen the edges. Fold one side of pastry over the filling, and seal edges firmly. Place on a dampened baking sheet. Brush with beaten egg and make two neat slits in the top of each one with a sharp knife. Bake at 220°C/425°F/gas mark 7 for 15 minutes, then at 180°C/350°F/gas mark 4 for a further 10 minutes. Serve hot or cold.

Rustic Sausage Rolls

*	Metric	Imperial	American
Al-bran cereal	25 g	1 oz	½ cup
Milk	60 ml	4 tbsp	4 tbsp
Self-raising (self-rising) flour	150 g	5 oz	1¼ cups
Salt and pepper			
Butter	40 g	1½ oz	3 tbsp
Grated, cheddar cheese	25 g	1 oz	¼ cup
French mustard	5 ml	1 tsp	1 tsp
Chipolata sausages	225 g	8 oz	½ lb

Put the bran into a bowl with the milk and leave to soak for 10 minutes. Sieve the flour, salt and pepper and rub in the butter. Stir in the cheese and soaked bran and knead well. Roll into a square. Spread the pastry with mustard and cut into 1 cm/½ in strips. Twist a strip of pastry round each sausage, overlapping the edges. If necessary, join two pieces of pastry so that the sausages are covered. Put on a greased baking sheet and bake at 220°C/425°F/gas mark 7 for 15 minutes. Serve hot or cold.

Special Sausage Rolls

*	*Metric*	*Imperial*	*American*
Puff pastry	*450 g*	*1 lb*	*1 lb*
Rashers (slices) streaky bacon	*8*	*8*	*8*
Mango chutney			
Large skinless pork sausages	*8*	*8*	*8*
Beaten egg for glaze			

Cut pastry in two and roll each piece to a strip 40 x 13 cm/16 x 5 in approximately. Stretch the bacon rashers with the flat blade of a knife and spread with chutney. Wrap each sausage in a rasher of bacon. Place four sausages end to end down each strip of pastry, brush the edge with beaten egg. Fold pastry over sausages, seal the edge well and knock up with the back of a knife. Cut each piece (between sausages) into four rolls. Place on a baking tray and brush with beaten egg. Make 2 or 3 slits in each. Bake at 220°C/425°F/gas mark 7 for 25 minutes. Serve hot or cold.

Eastern Ham Turnovers

*	Metric	Imperial	American
Shortcrust pastry	*450 g*	*1 lb*	*1 lb*
Cooked ham	*175 g*	*6 oz*	*3/8 lb*
Soured (dairy sour) cream	*45 ml*	*3 tbsp*	*3 tbsp*
Mayonnaise	*30 ml*	*2 tbsp*	*2 tbsp*
Pinch of salt			
Dry mustard	*1.5 ml*	*1/4 tsp*	*1/4 tsp*
Shake of cayenne pepper			
Curry powder	*5 ml*	*1 tsp*	*1 tsp*
Snipped fresh chives	*30 ml*	*2 tbsp*	*2 tbsp*
Beaten egg to glaze	*1*	*1*	*1*

Roll out the pastry 5 mm/1/4 in thick and cut into eighteen 7.5 cm/3 in rounds. Mince the ham or chop it finely, and mix in a bowl with cream, mayonnaise, seasonings and chives. Put 1 heaped 5 ml tsp of the mixture on one side of each pastry round. Moisten the edges of each round with water and fold over. Press the edges together firmly and prick the top of the turnovers with the tip of a sharp knife. Transfer to baking sheets. Brush with beaten egg to glaze. Bake at 220°C/425°F/gas mark 7 for 15 minutes until golden. Serve hot or cold.

Goat's Cheese and Leek Dreams

	Metric	*Imperial*	*American*
Leeks, chopped	*2*	*2*	*2*
Butter	*15 g*	*½ oz*	*1 tbsp*
Filo pastry sheets	*4*	*4*	*4*
Melted butter			
Goat cheese barrel (about 200 g), cut into 4 slices	*1*	*1*	*1*
Redcurrant jelly	*45 ml*	*3 tbsp*	*3 tbsp*
Orange juice	*30 ml*	*2 tbsp*	*2 tbsp*

Fry leeks gently in 15 g/½ oz butter for 2 minutes. Cover and 'sweat' over a gentle heat for 5 minutes or until soft but not brown. Lay sheets of pastry out on work surface and brush with a little melted butter. Fold in half to form squares. Brush with a little more butter. Divide cooked leeks between centres of squares. Top with a piece of cheese. Draw pastry up over filling gather together and squeeze to form parcels. Transfer to a buttered baking sheet and brush with a little more butter. Bake at 190°C/375°F/gas mark 5 for about 10 – 15 minutes until golden. Meanwhile melt redcurrant jelly and orange juice together. Serve cheese dreams on warm plates with the sauce spooned to one side.

Italian Cheese and Tomato Pies

	Metric	*Imperial*	*American*
Sheets filo pastry	*4*	*4*	*4*
Melted butter			
Tomatoes, chopped	*4*	*4*	*4*
Fontina cheese grated	*100 g*	*4 oz*	*1 cup*
Fresh basil or oregano, chopped	*20 ml*	*4 tsp*	*4 tsp*
A few capers, chopped (optional)			
Pepper			
Passata	*60 ml*	*4 tbsp*	*4 tbsp*
Garlic salt	*1.5 ml*	*¼ tsp*	*¼ tsp*
Fresh basil or oregano to garnish			

Lay filo on work surface. Brush each sheet with melted butter and fold in half to form squares. Brush with a little more butter. Divide chopped tomatoes between centres of squares. Top with cheese then herbs and capers (if using). Season with pepper. Carefully fold pastry over filling to form parcels. Transfer to a buttered baking sheet, folded sides down. Brush with a little more butter and bake at 190°C/375°F/gas mark 5 for about 10 minutes until golden. Meanwhile heat passata with garlic salt. Transfer pies to warm plates, spoon a little passata to one side and garnish with fresh herbs.

Crab and Cucumber Rolls

	Metric	*Imperial*	*American*
Small cucumber, finely diced	*1*	*1*	*1*
Button mushrooms, sliced	*50 g*	*2 oz*	*1 cup*
Butter	*25 g*	*1 oz*	*2 tbsp*
Plain (all-purpose) flour	*15 ml*	*1 tbsp*	*1 tbsp*
Fish or vegetable stock	*150 ml*	*¼ pt*	*⅔ cup*
Can white crab meat	*185 g*	*6 ½ oz*	*6 ½ oz*
Soy sauce	*5 ml*	*1 tsp*	*1 tsp*
Sherry	*10 ml*	*2 tsp*	*2 tsp*
Salt and pepper			
Sheets filo pastry	*4*	*4*	*4*
Melted butter			

Boil cucumber in lightly salted water for 3 minutes. Drain, rinse with cold water and drain well again. Fry mushrooms in butter for 3 minutes. Blend in flour then stock and bring to the boil, stirring all the time. Stir in cucumber, crab (with its juice), soy sauce, sherry and seasoning to taste. Leave to cool. Lay filo sheets on work surface and brush with a little melted butter and fold in half to form squares. Brush with a little more butter. Divide filling between squares, putting it to the centre of one edge. Fold in two sides over filling then roll up. Transfer to a buttered baking sheet and brush with a little more butter. Bake at 190°C/375°F/gas mark 5 for about 10 – 15 minutes. Serve warm. Alternatively, don't brush with butter but deep-fry in hot oil until crisp and golden then drain on kitchen paper before serving.

Prawn (Shrimp) Puffs

	Metric	*Imperial*	*American*
Choux pastry	*x 1*	*x 1*	*x 1*
Peeled prawns (shrimp)	*175 g*	*6 oz*	*1½ cups*
Mayonnaise	*60 ml*	*4 tbsp*	*4 tbsp*
Pinch of cayenne pepper			
Pepper			
Whipped (heavy) cream	*150 ml*	*¼ pt*	*⅔ cup*
Snipped fresh chives	*15 ml*	*1 tbsp*	*1 tbsp*

Divide choux pastry into six spoonsful and place well apart on a greased baking sheet. Bake at 220°C/425°F/gas mark 7 for 7 minutes then at 190°C/375°F/gas mark 5 for a further 15 minutes or until golden and puffy. Transfer to a wire rack and make a slit in the side of each to allow steam to escape. When cold roughly chop prawns and mix with mayonnaise and seasoning to taste. Fold in cream and chives and use to fill choux puffs. Chill until ready to serve.

Rooties

	Metric	*Imperial*	*American*
Shortcrust pastry	*450 g*	*1 lb*	*1 lb*
Caraway seeds	*15 ml*	*1 tbsp*	*1 tbsp*
Carrots, diced small	*2*	*2*	*2*
Medium potato, diced small	*1*	*1*	*1*
Small swede (rutabaga), diced small	½	½	½
Onion, chopped	*1*	*1*	*1*
Small parsnip or sweet potato, diced small	*1*	*1*	*1*
Salt and pepper			
Yeast extract	*5 ml*	*1 tsp*	*1 tsp*
Boiling water	*30 ml*	*2 tbsp*	*2 tbsp*
Egg, beaten	*1*	*1*	*1*

Roll out pastry and cut into four 18 cm/7 in rounds. Sprinkle each with caraway seeds and roll in lightly with rolling pin.

Mix vegetables together and season well. Divide among centres of pastry. Mix yeast extract and water and spoon over. Brush edges with beaten egg. Draw up over filling and crimp between fingers and thumb, pressing edges well together to seal.

Transfer to a baking sheet, brush with beaten egg then bake at 190°C/375°F/gas mark 5 for about 45 minutes until cooked through. Serve warm or cold.

Tuna and Sweetcorn Pies

*	Metric	Imperial	American
Shortcrust pastry	750 g	1½ lb	1½ lb
Rashers (slices) streaky bacon	4	4	4
Butter	15 g	½ oz	1 tbsp
Medium onion, finely chopped	1	1	1
Can tuna fish	185 g	6 ½ oz	6 ½ oz
Sweetcorn kernels	175 g	6 oz	1½ cups
Salt and pepper			
Tomatoes	3	3	3
Beaten egg to glaze			

Fry bacon in pan without fat until crisp, then remove. Add butter to pan and cook onion gently until soft. Drain tuna. Mix all filling ingredients together except tomatoes. Cut off one-third of pastry and keep for lids. Roll out remaining two-thirds and cut into twelve 10 cm/4 in circles. Use to line deep foil baking cases about 7.5 cm/3 in across. Half-fill with tuna mixture, add tomato slices and cover with remaining filling. Roll out remaining pastry and cut into circles for lids. Dampen edges of pies, cover with lids and seal well. Make a small hole in centre of each pie. Brush with beaten egg. Bake at 190°C/375°F/gas mark 5 for 40 minutes until pastry is golden brown. Serve hot or cold

Savoury Meat Pasties

*	*Metric*	*Imperial*	*American*
Shortcrust pastry	*450 g*	*1 lb*	*1 lb*
Raw minced (ground) beef	*225 g*	*8 oz*	*½ lb*
Streaky bacon, chopped	*175 g*	*6 oz*	*⅜ lb*
Lambs' kidneys, chopped	*100 g*	*4 oz*	*¼ lb*
Large onion, finely chopped	*1*	*1*	*1*
Salt and pepper			
Worcestershire sauce	*2.5 ml*	*½ tsp*	*½ tsp*
Beaten egg to glaze			

Roll out the pastry and cut it into six 18 cm/7 in rounds. Mix the beef, bacon, kidney, onion, seasoning and sauce. Put the mixture on to half of each round, brush edge with beaten egg and fold over pastry. Pinch the edges together and brush with beaten egg to glaze. Bake at 220°C/425°F/gas mark 7 for 15 minutes, and then at 180°C/350°F/gas mark 4 for 45 minutes. Serve hot or cold.

Luncheon Squares

*	Metric	Imperial	American
Shortcrust pastry	350 g	12 oz	¾ lb
Medium onion, chopped finely	1	1	1
Medium potato, chopped finely	1	1	1
Oil	30 ml	2 tbsp	2 tbsp
Canned luncheon meat, cubed	225 g	8 oz	½ lb
White sauce	150 ml	¼ pt	⅔ cup
Chopped fresh parsley	5 ml	1 tsp	1 tsp
Grated lemon rind	5 ml	1 tsp	1 tsp
Salt and pepper			

Roll out the pastry and use half to line a 20 cm/8 in square sandwich tin. Fry onion and potato in hot oil until just soft. Drain off surplus oil. Mix the onion and potato with the meat, sauce, parsley, lemon rind, salt and pepper. Put into the pastry case and cover with the remaining pastry. Bake at 220°C/425°F/gas mark 7 for 15 minutes, then at 180°C/350°F/gas mark 4 for 15 minutes. Cut into nine squares to serve hot or cold.

Turkey Tartlets

	Metric	*Imperial*	*American*
Shortcrust pastry	*350 g*	*12 oz*	*¾ lb*
Onion, chopped	*1*	*1*	*1*
Butter	*25 g*	*1 oz*	*2 tbsp*
Can apricot halves, drained	*425 g*	*15 oz*	*15 oz*
Curry paste	*10 ml*	*2 tsp*	*2 tsp*
Lemon juice	*10 ml*	*2 tsp*	*2 tsp*
Soured (dairy sour) cream	*150 ml*	*¼ pt*	*⅔ cup*
Cooked turkey, chopped	*275 g*	*10 oz*	*⅝ lb*
Tabasco	*2.5 ml*	*½ tsp*	*½ tsp*
Salt and pepper			
Frozen peas	*100 g*	*4 oz*	*1 cup*
Beaten egg to glaze			

Cook the onion in butter until golden. Add the apricots. Simmer for 20 minutes until reduced to a thick pulp. Thin the curry paste with a little water and add to the apricots with lemon juice. Stir in the soured cream and turkey. Bring to the boil, simmer gently for 10 minutes. Add the Tabasco and season to taste. Remove from heat, stir in peas, leave to cool.

Roll out one half of pastry and use to line individual patty tins. Divide the filling equally between the tarts. Roll out remaining pastry and use for 'lids'. Brush with beaten egg. Press lids in place. Pinch the edges together with thumb and forefinger and decorate tops with pastry ‘leaves’. Glaze with beaten egg. Cook at 220°C/425°F/gas mark 7 for 20 minutes. Serve hot or cold.

SAVOURY PUDDINGS

Suet pastry is a traditional winter favourite. It may be used as a complete casing for the filling in a basin, just as a top crust, or to roll round a filling, rather like a Swiss roll.

To make a suet crust (if you want to make up your own recipes) allow 25 g/1 oz/¼ cup self-raising flour to 15 g/½ oz/1 tbsp shredded (chopped) suet for one helping of pudding. For a family-sized (4 – 5 person) pudding, allow 225 g/8 oz/2 cups flour to 100 g/4 oz/1 cup suet, which will allow for some second helpings. For whatever sized pudding you need, always allow half as much suet as flour. Add a pinch of salt and enough cold water to give a soft but not sticky dough.

To cover a pudding, use kitchen foil or double greaseproof paper brushed with oil, or a pudding cloth. When wrapping roly-poly puddings, greaseproof paper covered with foil will be satisfactory, or a lightly floured pudding cloth. Tie the ends of the pudding with string, allowing room for expansion. When covering a pudding in a basin, put a pleat in the covering so the top crust can expand. Put the pudding into a pan of boiling water to come about halfway up the basin, or immerse a long pudding. Cover and keep the pan on medium heat so that the water bubbles gently. Top up with boiling water as necessary.

You will also find other delicious savoury puddings using bread or potato instead of suet crust.

Steak and Kidney Pudding

*	Metric	Imperial	American
Stewing steak	*450 g*	*1 lb*	*1 lb*
Ox kidney	*100 g*	*4 oz*	*¼ lb*
Onion, chopped	*1*	*1*	*1*
Suet crust	*350 g*	*12 oz*	*¾ lb*
Salt and pepper			
Beef stock	*90 ml*	*6 tbsp*	*6 tbsp*

Cut steak into thin pieces and chop kidney into small pieces. Mix with the onion. Make suet pastry. Line a greased basin with two-thirds of the pastry. Put in the meat, and season well with salt and pepper and add a sprinkling of flour. Add stock almost to the top of the basin. Cover with remaining pastry and seal edges. Cover and steam for 4 hours. Serve hot.

Variations: 50 g/2 oz/1 cup chopped mushrooms may be added.

Bacon Roll

	Metric	*Imperial*	*American*
Suet crust	*350 g*	*12 oz*	*¾ lb*
Salt and pepper			
Chopped mixed bacon and onion	*175 g*	*6 oz*	*⅜ lb*
Passata	*300 ml*	*½ pt*	*1 ¼ cups*

Make suet pastry. Roll into a rectangle and put on bacon and onion, and plenty of seasoning. A little chopped sage may be added. Roll up like a Swiss roll in a floured cloth and boil for 1½ hours. Serve sliced with hot passata spooned over.

Somerset Pudding

*	*Metric*	*Imperial*	*American*
Suet crust	*450 g*	*1lb*	*1lb*
Chicken	*1.75 kg*	*4 lb*	*4 lb*
Medium onion, chopped	*1*	*1*	*1*
Garlic clove, chopped	*1*	*1*	*1*
Salt and pepper			
Chopped fresh parsley	*15 ml*	*1 tbsp*	*1 tbsp*
Chopped fresh thyme	*10 ml*	*2 tsp*	*2 tsp*
Cider	*150 ml*	*¼ pt*	*⅔ cup*

Make suet pastry. Line a large basin with two-thirds of the pastry. Skin the chicken and cut flesh from the wings, legs and breast and cut into small pieces. Simmer carcass in enough water to cover for 1 hour to make stock. Put alternate layers of chicken, onion and garlic into the basin. Season layers with salt, pepper and herbs. Cover with cider made up to 300 ml/½ pt/1¼ cups with chicken stock. Cover with remaining pastry. Cover and steam for 4 hours. Serve hot with more chicken stock, or with parsley sauce.

Brunswick Pudding

*	*Metric*	*Imperial*	*American*
Suet crust	*350 g*	*12 oz*	*¾ lb*
Salt and pepper			
White wine	*90 ml*	*6 tbsp*	*6 tbsp*
Small rabbit, boned and diced	*1*	*1*	*1*
Chopped fresh sage	*2.5 ml*	*½ tsp*	*½ tsp*
Onion, sliced	*1*	*1*	*1*
Tomatoes, sliced	*2*	*2*	*2*
Mushrooms, chopped	*50 g*	*2 oz*	*½ cup*
Sweetcorn	*100 g*	*4 oz*	*1 cup*

Make suet pastry, and use two-thirds of it to line a greased basin. Fill pudding with rabbit , wine, sage, onions, tomatoes, mushrooms and sweetcorn. Season to taste. Cover with remaining pastry. Cover and steam for 4 hours. Serve hot.

Kidney Dumpling

	Metric	Imperial	American
Suet crust	*350 g*	*12 oz*	*¾ lb*
Lamb's kidneys	*4*	*4*	*4*
Large onions	*4*	*4*	*4*
Salt and pepper			

Make up suet pastry. Roll out in a square and cut four 15 cm/6 in squares. Skin the kidneys and remove cores. Peel the onions and scoop out the centres. Season inside the onion centres and put a kidney in each one. Put an onion on to each pastry square and pinch up the corners to enclose the onions completely. Turn upside down on a baking sheet so that the joins come underneath. Bake at 180°C/350°F/gas mark 4 for 1¼ hours. Lift carefully off the baking sheet and serve hot with gravy.

Pork and Sausage Pudding

*	Metric	Imperial	American
Suet crust	350 g	12 oz	¾ lb
Lean pork	750 g	1½ lb	1½ lb
Pork sausagemeat	350 g	12 oz	¾ lb
Sage leaves	6	6	6
Medium onion, finely chopped	1	1	1
Salt and pepper			
Cider or apple juice	90 ml	6 tbsp	6 tbsp

Make suet pastry. Line a basin with two-thirds of the pastry. Cut the pork in small thin slices. Shape the sausagemeat into small balls. Layer the meats, sage, onion, salt and pepper. Add cider or apple juice. Cover with the remaining pastry. Cover and boil for 4 hours. Serve hot.

Pork, Leek and Apple Pudding

*	Metric	Imperial	American
Suet crust	*350 g*	*12 oz*	*¾ lb*
Fresh lean pork, diced	*225 g*	*8 oz*	*½ lb*
Medium cooking apple chopped	*1*	*1*	*1*
Salt and pepper			
Leeks, chopped	*2*	*2*	*2*
Pork or chicken stock	*90 ml*	*6 tbsp*	*6 tbsp*
Chopped fresh sage	*2.5 ml*	*½ tsp*	*½ tsp*

Make suet pastry. Line basin with two-thirds of pastry, and put in pork, apple, leeks, salt and pepper, sage and stock. Put on pastry lid, cover and boil for 4 hours. Serve hot

Bacon Layer Pudding

	Metric	*Imperial*	*American*
Suet crust	*225 g*	*8 oz*	*½ lb*
Bacon, chopped	*225 g*	*8 oz*	*½ lb*
Medium onions, grated	*2*	*2*	*2*
Medium carrots, grated	*2*	*2*	*2*
Chopped cooked spinach	*225 g*	*8 oz*	*½ lb*

Make up suet pastry. Roll out thinly and cut a round to fit the bottom of a greased 1.2 litre/2 pt/5 cup pudding basin. Put a layer of bacon on the pastry and top with a little onion, carrot and spinach. Top with another layer of pastry. Continue these layers until the basin is full, topping with pastry. Cover and steam for 2 hours. Serve hot with fresh tomato sauce or passata.

Note. For a more solid pudding, use 350 g/12 oz/ ¾ lb pastry

Liver and Bacon Dumpling

	Metric	*Imperial*	*American*
Suet crust	*450 g*	*1 lb*	*1 lb*
Pig's liver, chopped small	*225 g*	*8 oz*	*½ lb*
Streaky bacon, chopped small	*225 g*	*8 oz*	*½ lb*
Large onions, grated	*2*	*2*	*2*
Chopped fresh sage	*10 ml*	*2 tsp*	*2 tsp*
Salt and pepper			

Make suet pastry. Roll out to a rectangle. Spread liver and bacon over the suet pastry. Top with onions and sprinkle with sage, salt and pepper. Roll up tightly like a Swiss roll and tie in a floured cloth. Boil for 2½ hours. Serve hot with gravy.

Cheese and Potato Pudding with Leek Sauce

	Metric	*Imperial*	*American*
Potatoes, peeled and diced	*450 g*	*1 lb*	*1 lb*
Butter	*50 g*	*2 oz*	*¼ cup*
Eggs	*3*	*3*	*3*
Milk	*60 ml*	*4 tbsp*	*4 tbsp*
Cheddar cheese, grated	*100 g*	*4 oz*	*1 cup*
Made mustard	*2.5 ml*	*½ tsp*	*½ tsp*
Salt and pepper			
Leeks, chopped	*3*	*3*	*3*
Milk	*300 ml*	*½ pt*	*1 ¼ cups*

Grease and flour a 1.2 litre/2 pt/5 cup pudding basin. Cook potatoes in boiling salted water until tender. Drain and mash with butter. Separate eggs and beat yolks into potatoes with milk. Stir in the cheese, mustard and a little salt and pepper. Whisk egg whites until stiff and fold into mixture with a metal spoon. Turn into basin, cover and steam for 40 minutes.

Meanwhile cook leeks in milk for about 15 minutes until tender. Purée in a processor or pass through a sieve. Return to pan, season and re-heat. Turn pudding out onto a warm dish and serve straight away with the sauce.

Cheesey Bread and Butter Pudding

	Metric	Imperial	American
Butter	*50 g*	*2 oz*	*¼ cup*
Garlic clove, crushed	*1*	*1*	*1*
Dried mixed herbs	*2.5 ml*	*½ tsp*	*½ tsp*
Slices bread	*8*	*8*	*8*
Eggs	*4*	*4*	*4*
Milk	*300 ml*	*½ pt*	*1 ¼ cups*
Salt and pepper			
Peas	*100 g*	*4 oz*	*1 cup*
Cheddar cheese, grated	*175 g*	*6 oz*	*1 ½ cups*

Mix butter with garlic and herbs. Spread on bread and lay half the slices, buttered side down in an ovenproof dish. Beat eggs with milk, stir in a little salt and pepper, the peas and cheese. Pour half the mixture into a dish. Top with remaining bread and egg mixture. Bake at 200°C/400°F/gas mark 6 for about 30 – 40 minutes until golden and set. Serve hot.

Savoury Summer Pudding

	Metric	Imperial	American
Tomatoes, skinned and chopped	450 g	1 lb	1 lb
Carrots, grated	225 g	8 oz	½ lb
Courgettes (zucchini), grated	225 g	8 oz	½ lb
Medium (white) turnip, grated	1	1	1
Red (bell) pepper, finely chopped	1	1	1
Medium onion, finely chopped	1	1	1
Butter	50 g	2 oz	¼ cup
Chopped mixed fresh herbs	15 ml	1 tbsp	1 tbsp
Salt and pepper			
Pinch of caster (superfine) sugar			
Slices bread	8	8	8
Fromage frais or quark,			
Chopped fresh parsley to garnish			

Put prepared vetetables in a pan with the butter, herbs, a little salt and pepper and the sugar. Cook stirring for 2 minutes, then cover and cook gently for 10 minutes. Meanwhile, trim crusts off bread and use 6 slices to line a 1.2 litre/2 pt/5 cup pudding basin. Stand basin on a plate to catch any drips. Spoon cooked vegetables into basin.

Use remaining slices of bread to cover top, trimming the last one to fit neatly into the gaps. Cover with greaseproof paper then a small plate or saucer, placing a heavy weight on top. Chill overnight.

To serve: loosen edge with a round bladed knife and turn out onto a plate. Spoon some fromage frais or quark on top and sprinkle with chopped parsley.

INDEX